HOW SHOULD
CHRISTIANS
RESPOND?

The
WAR
on Terror

Nick Solly Megoran

Foreword by David W. Augsburger

IVP Books

An imprint of InterVarsity Press
Downers Grove, Illinois

InterVarsity Press
P.O. Box 1400, Downers Grove, IL 60515-1426
Internet: www.ivpress.com
E-mail: email@ivpress.com

InterVarsity Press® is the book-publishing division of InterVarsity Christian Fellowship/U.S.A®, a student movement active on campus at hundreds of universities, colleges and schools of nursing in the United States of America, and a member movement of the International Fellowship of Evangelical Students. For information about local and regional activities, write Public Relations Dept., InterVarsity Christian Fellowship/U.S.A., 6400 Schroeder Rd., P.O. Box 7895, Madison, WI 53707-7895, or visit the IVCF website at <www.intervarsity.org>.

Cover design: Janelle Cipriano
Cover image: Ghaith Abdul-Ahad/Getty Images

ISBN 978-0-8308-3487-7

Printed in the United States of America ∞

Library of Congress Cataloging-in-Publication Data

Megoran, Nick Solly.
  The war on terror: how should Christians respond? / Nick Solly
Megoran.
       p. cm.
  Includes bibliographical references.
  ISBN 978-0-8308-3487-7 (pbk.: alk. paper)
  1. War—Religious aspects—Christianity. 2. Terrorism—Religious
aspects—Christianity. I. Title.
  BT736.2.M392007
  261.8'73—dc22
                                                              2007026868

| P | 19 | 18 | 17 | 16 | 15 | 14 | 13 | 12 | 11 | 10 | 9 | 8 | 7 | 6 | 5 | 4 | 3 | 2 | 1 |
| Y | 23 | 22 | 21 | 20 | 19 | 18 | 17 | 16 | 15 | 14 | 13 | 12 | 11 | 10 | 09 | 08 | 07 |

To Nick Ladd, a godly mentor,

and to Emily Rose Lola,
that she may grow up after his example.

Contents

Foreword

The British-American "war on terror" has offered us again the opportunity to learn the lesson we do not learn—what we hate, we recreate; what we fear, we mirror; what we fight, we repeat.

Nick Solly Megoran has written a prophetic analysis of this dark repetition compulsion that is the shadow of human history. Many books praise prophets, but with faint praise when they fail to be prophetic. Megoran risks facing unappreciative audiences and unapplauded truth.

In *The War on Terror* he does not hesitate to look at how the response from the West has validated its stated motivations rather than reduced the conflict. (Question: Is it a war? If terror is the enemy, why are terror, shock and awe its primary means?) Megoran writes from between the traditions—one line moves from the Gospels, through such persons as Peter, Paul, the early church fathers, St. Francis, Menno Simons, Henry Martyn, André and Magda Trocmé, George Bell, and so on; the other from Constantine through Ambrose, Augustine, the crusades, the Reformation, the Inquisition, Pius XII, the silent churches of Europe under the Nazis, and on and on to today. Megoran walks this torturous line while asking which responses have been faithful to Jesus and which betray his central mission and words.

This is a book for personal study, for group discussion, for quoting from the pulpit, for any place willing to explore a prophetic answer to issues that have been receiving loud silence from Christians for too long.

David W. Augsburger
Professor of Pastoral Care and Conflict Studies
Fuller Theological Seminary

Acknowledgments

I would like to acknowledge the congregations of St. Barnabas Church, Ditchburn Place and Sidney Sussex College Chapel, Cambridge, for their prayerful support and encouragement; also Nick Ladd, Rachel and Richard Rhodes James, and Peter Waddell, for extending invitations to preach to them. I am grateful to Rachel Solly Megoran, who has been supportive and insightful. I also appreciated the help of Cathy Nobles of the Reconciliation Walk, the encouragement of Eleanor Trotter and Kate Byrom of Inter-Varsity Press, and the insights of anonymous referees that helped to improve this book enormously. I would like to thank Christy Risser, who introduced me to the idea that Christians are people who live with two passports. My thanks also to Roger Fay of the *Evangelical Times* for allowing me to use material about Henry Martyn in chapter 4 from my article "Henry Martyn: Iraq—Lessons in a Time of War," which originally appeared in the *Evangelical Times*, March 2003, page 14.

PART 1

SETTING THE SCENE

1

Introduction

In March 2003, on the eve of the U.S. invasion of Iraq, a group of Iraqi church workers wrote a harrowing open letter to fellow Christians in America. "Every day we thank God for being alive because we do not know what tomorrow has hidden for us," they said. "The nightmare of the new war is haunting us always and everywhere," they continued, imploring their American brothers and sisters in Christ not to compound their suffering by launching another attack on their homeland.

If the Iraqi Christians expected that Western believers would unite to support them, they were tragically mistaken. Although the war's most prominent critics included the archbishop of Canterbury, the pope and evangelical leaders from around the world, its major architects, President George W. Bush and former British prime minister Tony Blair, were also well known for their Christian faith. While the U.S. National Council of Churches led prayers for peace, other churches organized prayer campaigns in support of the war, and one American prayer network called for "cruise and scud prayers" against Iraq to speed the U.S. victory. Although these sharp divisions arguably damaged the reputation of Christianity, the real cost to the church was in the large numbers of Christians, mainly American and Iraqi, who died in Iraq itself—sometimes killed by fellow believers belonging to the "other side." Their plight, and indeed the plight of all Iraqis, has turned this desperate letter on the eye of the war into a question that haunts the Western Christian church—how should we have replied to them?

President Bush himself was clear: he justified the invasion of Iraq by linking it to the attacks on New York and Washington on September 11, 2001, and the danger of further attacks if Iraq acquired "weapons of mass destruction." Since then, Christians have been forced to confront the question of how we are to respond to the War on Terror, a question made more complicated by the open divisions in the church on the issue. Subsequent incidents directly or indirectly related to that fateful Tuesday have reinforced the urgency of this: from the U.S.-led invasions of Afghanistan in 2002 and Iraq in 2003, to Islamist suicide bomb attacks against public transport in Madrid on March 11, 2004, and London on July 7, 2005. (Unsuccessful plots, such as the alleged Islamist attempt to blow up airliners taking off from Britain that was foiled in August 2006, have further underlined how pressing this topic is.)

These events inevitably raise many questions for us. Where was God on 9/11, 7/7, and when the bombs started falling on Afghanistan and Iraq? Why does God allow wars and terrorist attacks to happen? Should Western Christians support or oppose their governments' wars? Should Palestinian and Iraqi Christians support armed resistance to the occupation of their lands? Of what relevance is the gospel to the big international political questions of our day? Is there a distinctive message that the church can proclaim at this time? How can the Bible guide our thinking and help us live out our daily lives in the War on Terror? Do the Old and New Testaments contradict each other in what they teach about how we should treat our enemies? Was Jesus seriously commanding us to "love our enemies," even when they are suicide bombers or enemy soldiers? What can ordinary Christians do, and how should we pray for the world?

ANSWERING DIFFICULT QUESTIONS

The questions posed by the War on Terror are vitally important. Because they have made such an impact on public consciousness and daily life, no Christian can avoid them, and this book is intended to provide readers with biblical insights to enable them to begin to answer these questions for themselves. It is written from the conviction that the questions raised by the War on Terror are among the most important of our age, but that their consideration should be rooted in a life of Christian worship that is fed by reflection on Scripture.

THE BIBLE AND THE WORLD

Chapters three through ten of this book are expositions of Scripture, rooted in the evangelical tradition. I affirm that the Bible is the revealed Word of God that exists primarily to point humankind to salvation by faith in the gospel of Christ and to holy lives worthy of that calling. I consider the War on Terror in relation to this. It is hoped that the reader will be equipped not merely to think about war, but will also be spiritually built up in their faith in Christ and better enabled to witness to the gospel by talking sensibly to non-Christians in the context of discussions about war.

I am not an academic theologian by training but a political geographer, which is reflected in this book. I have spent much of the past decade conducting research on nationalism, violence and peace in the Islamic world. More recently, I have worked on the politics of the War on Terror and church responses to it. During this time I have traveled widely in Muslim countries. My study of practical problems in these fraught contexts has led me to an increasingly strong conviction that the Bible is the most practical book ever written, and that a violent and warring world is simply crying out for real Christianity. At the same time, my involvement with Christian minorities in Muslim countries has sensitized me to their concerns and plight. Whenever we talk about how "we" as Christians should respond to the War on Terror, we ought to recall that that "we" includes Palestinians, Iraqis and others as well as Britons and Americans. A key theme in this book is that the church, created by God of all those saved in Christ Jesus, is our primary community of belonging, our primary citizenship.

This book began life as a number of sermons preached in Cambridge, U.K. As part of the normal cycle of church worship, they were intended to assist people to encounter God by proclaiming his salvation. However, they tended to occur at times such as the anniversary of the September 11 attacks, the invasion of Iraq and the London bombs, and my set texts were also peculiarly appropriate to the subject of the War on Terror. Because of this, I had to address questions that my congregations faced, the questions listed on pages 16-17. Their positive responses and the encouragement of other Christians who read the texts persuaded me to write this book.

WHAT DOES THE BIBLE SAY ABOUT WAR?

One of the twentieth century's greatest British evangelical preachers, Martyn Lloyd-Jones, taught during the German Blitz on London in World War II that war is a manifestation (an example, a symptom) and a consequence of sin, for which humanity as a race must bear responsibility.[1] However, God has not left us by ourselves to sort out this mess. By Christ's death and resurrection, every man, woman and child, through repentance and faith in Christ, may know forgiveness of sins, peace with God and the transforming power of his Holy Spirit in their lives. But that must not stop at a mere inner change. What Paul calls "the gospel of peace"—the creation in Christ of a new nation of people made up from every human nation—has relevance to every aspect of human life, including war and terrorism in the twenty-first century.

OUTLINE

The key conviction of this book is, therefore, that the Christian gospel, as revealed in the Bible and testified to by the church, is God's glorious answer to the violence that sinful humanity has wreaked upon the world.

Although each chapter can be read individually as an exposition of Scripture, the book is divided into three parts that develop an overall argument. This first part sets the book in the context of recent events and Christian responses to them. The second part, "War and Peace," addresses the "big questions"—why war happens, what our response should be and how this is all grounded in the great biblical doctrines of salvation by grace. Having established this, the chapters in the third part, "Citizens of Heaven," explore some practical aspects of this at greater length. These include being citizens of heaven and also citizens of warring states, how to learn the skills of peacemaking, and how ordinary Christians have transformed violent situations by obedient faith in Christ. Chapters seven and eight look at war in the New and Old Testaments, and how being citizens of heaven changed with the first coming of Christ. All of these chapters, to some degree or another, indicate that the gospel brings hope to a violent world. The final part, "Christian Hope and the War on Terror," brings out the theme of hope more explicitly. It is recommended that the relevant biblical passage be read prayerfully before starting each chapter.

In addition there are three study guides. They are accessible introductions to the general reader and assume no expertise in these fields, but they should also help to clarify and summarize arguments for people with more knowledge. Recommended reading, questions and suggestions are provided to help with both individual and church group study. Finally, a short list of ideas is included for churches to take this further.

GOSPEL WITNESS IN WARTIME

As war clouds gathered over Europe in 1939, Anglican bishop George Bell wrote a remarkable essay asking what the church's function in wartime was.[2] He argued simply that, "it is the function of the Church at all costs to remain the Church" and "preach the gospel of Christ." There is no separate gospel for wartime and peacetime, he explained, and the church must not take one side or the other when conflict begins. In emotionally charged climates of hatred, fear, retaliation and nationalist fervor, that may not be an easy position to adhere to. Bishop Bell admitted this himself: "The Church may have a difficult task in wartime. But it has an extraordinary opportunity." The War on Terror is just such an opportunity for Christians confidently and intelligently to proclaim their gospel to the world, whether that is in national debates, over coffee-break discussions with coworkers, over dinner with friends, during university seminars or on the school playground. It is my hope and prayer that this book will enable Christians to do just that.

2

What Is Terrorism and the War on Terror?

In 2003 it was reported in the news that a twelve-year-old boy in a Louisiana diner joked to his friends, "I'm gonna get you" if they ate all the potatoes first. The police were called and promptly charged the boy with making "terroristic threats." He was incarcerated for two weeks before his trial.

This reaction of an overzealous police officer might be amusing, but it highlights a question that has been intensely debated by scholars of the subject: what, exactly, is "terrorism"? In popular imagination, two images of "terrorism" can commonly be identified. In British and American contexts these tend to fall along political lines. For those on the right wing, "terrorism" is a tactic whereby evil members of shadowy, nongovernmental organizations, driven by irrational hatred or vengeance and a desire to express their frustration, create a climate of fear by trying to kill, at random, as many innocent civilians as possible. They pursue this end by misusing the products of modern technology, detonating bombs in trains and buses, hijacking airplanes, and shooting into crowds in cities. As someone who narrowly missed such an attack as a boy in London, this was the understanding of terrorism that I grew up with. It is largely the definition used by U.S. and U.K. leaders to describe violence such as that seen in New York on September 11, 2001.

An alternative popular image, especially favored by elements of the political left, is that "terrorism" as defined above is, in some cases, the understandable but misguided resistance by poor people to oppressive governments, who are the real terrorists. According to this theory, governments that push the marginalized into impossible situations of poverty and repression themselves create the circumstances whereby hopeless people are driven into desperate acts of resistance. Members of such resistance groups are labeled "terrorists" by governments but are actually "freedom fighters" struggling for justice. Proponents of this position note that men once described as "terrorists" by Western governments, such as Nelson Mandela of South Africa and Gerry Adams of Northern Ireland, have subsequently been feted as legitimate politicians. This position has been epitomized by British antiwar politician George Galloway. He has called President Bush and Tony Blair the world's top "terrorists" for bombing Afghanistan and Iraq, and he created controversy in May 2006 by saying that it would be justifiable for a suicide bomber to kill Blair.

WHAT IS THE WAR ON TERROR?

The War on Terror is used by President George W. Bush to describe that element of his foreign and domestic policy formulated in response to the attacks of September 11, 2001. On that day, nineteen men hijacked four passenger planes on internal flights in the United States. Two planes careered into the World Trade Center, causing its iconic Twin Towers to collapse. The third was flown into the Pentagon in Washington, D.C., and a fourth crashed into a field when passengers, who learned via cell phones what had happened to the other planes, overpowered the hijackers. Around 3,000 people were killed in the world's worst single attack by a nonstate terrorist organization. The hijackers were of Saudi Arabian and Egyptian origin, linked to Osama bin Laden's al-Qaeda network, which purported to seek to drive Americans out of the Middle East. They had been planning the elaborate operation for years.

In response, President Bush launched two major wars. Afghanistan was invaded in October 2001 to capture bin Laden and topple the hard-line Islamic Taliban government that President Bush alleged was sheltering him. In March 2003, the United States invaded Iraq to overthrow President Saddam Hussein who, U.S. leaders alleged, was preparing illegal "weapons of mass destruction" that could potentially be given to its allies such as al-Qaeda for future attacks on the United States. Neither action was authorized at the time by the United Nations Security Council, although the United States built coalitions in each case to provide military, political and logistical support. Both of these episodes, particularly the Iraq invasion, were controversial and generated considerable opposition at home and abroad. They also led to major realignments of American foreign policy, as when the United States opened military bases with new allies in the War on Terror such as Uzbekistan, Kyrgyzstan and Pakistan, and distanced itself from former allies such as France and Germany, who were increasingly critical of its foreign policy.

In Iraq itself, the abuse of detainees at Abu Ghraib and other prisons damaged America's reputation, but U.S. leaders insisted that such instances were isolated and not part of official policy. The failure to find either Osama bin Laden in Afghanistan or the "weapons of mass destruction" in Iraq led many to question both the capability and motives of the U.S.-led coalitions. At the same time, the foiling of violent plots by Islamists in countries such as the U.K., Canada and Australia served as reminders that genuine dangers were faced. Dramatic and fatal attacks on allies of America in Madrid, London and Bali were tragic demonstrations that counterterrorist measures could not always anticipate or prevent such attacks.

Domestic aspects of the War on Terror likewise proved controversial. New laws were enacted to increase state antiterrorism powers, and measures to combat terrorism that bypassed the high standards of Western domestic laws were introduced, such as the detention without trial of suspected terrorists in Guantanamo Bay, Cuba, and the "extraordinary rendition" (kidnapping and transportation) to third countries of others. These developments and debates were mirrored in countries such as Britain and Australia, who supported President Bush militarily and enacted similar laws at home. The War on Terror also led to shifts of power between different U.S. government departments, as ideological rivalries over the direction of U.S. foreign policy were played out between factions in the Bush administration and the military. These developments proved highly contentious within the United States, but of less interest in other countries.

President Bush and his supporters insisted that the United States needed new ways to defend itself, and democracy, against a new and insidious threat. They also argued that elections in Afghanistan and Iraq following the invasions have laid the foundation for model democratic governments in the regions. Critics of the War on Terror argued that America's wars created massive damage and loss of life without significantly disrupting terrorist networks, breeding an anger that could backfire in greater support for bin Laden. They also argued that domestic legislation that eroded civil liberties, and foreign support of undemocratic regimes in countries such as Uzbekistan, Pakistan and Saudi Arabia, morally undermined the case that the United States was making for democracy.

It is impossible to judge if America is "winning" the War on Terror, nor is it even clear how that could be ascertained. President

Bush, Tony Blair and their supporters point to elections in Afghanistan and Iraq where once there was tyranny, and the arrests of numerous men plotting further attacks around the world. Critics observe that violence and chaos is ongoing in Afghanistan and Iraq, that the number of anti-Western Islamist terrorist incidents has skyrocketed since 2001, and that the War on Terror has radicalized large sections of Muslim opinion around the world against the United States and its allies. What cannot be denied is that the War on Terror has been the defining political drama in countries such as the U.S., the U.K., Afghanistan, Iraq and elsewhere, and that Christians in all these countries have therefore been obliged to reflect on it in the light of their faith in Jesus Christ and the guidance of Scripture.

It is valuable to consider how the chief protagonists of the War on Terror—Osama bin Laden and George W. Bush—have explained to the world their understanding of why they are fighting. Osama bin Laden and George W. Bush both see the war as moral (good versus evil), although bin Laden stresses political and spiritual factors far more than Bush does. (See Study Guide 1 for a description of how a number of well-known political analysts have written about this topic.)

Osama bin Laden. In a "letter to the American people" of November 2002, Osama bin Laden explained his understanding of the War on Terror. It opened and closed with quotes from the Qur'an, calling on Muslims to fight unbelievers and promising eternal rewards for those who die in the process. Its main body addressed two questions. bin Laden's answer to "why are we fighting and opposing you?" was simply, "because you attacked us and continue to attack us." bin Laden cited the British and American roles in the creation and support of Israel and the subjugation of Palestinians, as well as American support of Russian atrocities against Chech-

nya, Indian oppression of Kashmir, and backing of corrupt and oppressive regimes in Muslim states. He accused the U.S. of the theft
of oil wealth at low prices and a lack of care for the suffering of
Iraqi children under U.S. sanctions. He also charged the U.S. with
hypocrisy for allowing Israel to develop "weapons of mass destruction" yet forbidding others (meaning Iraq) to do the same. He
railed against the presence of the U.S. military in Muslim lands. Bin
Laden gave a lengthy explanation of why he considered it justified
to attack American civilians. He argued that, as taxpayers and citizens, the American people as a whole had responsibility for the actions of their government but had not tried to change them.

This is a variant of "just-war" reasoning (see p. 30), arguing that
he is essentially fighting a war of defense. Bin Laden also posed a
second question: "What do we want from you?" His first response
was that he wanted conversion to Islam and Islamic (shari'a) law,
which would lead to general cultural transformation. He called on
America to end fornication, homosexuality, drinking of alcohol,
gambling and trading with interest, accusing it of being "the worst
civilization witnessed by the history of mankind." He also called on
America to sign the Kyoto agreement on climate change and end
the destruction of the planet by greedy industries, as well as to stop
the supposed control of political parties and the media by wealthy
businessmen, especially Jews. He demanded that the U.S. end double standards by not supporting dictators in the Muslim world or
states oppressing Muslims, especially Israel. He concluded his "letter" by warning the Americans that if they did not withdraw, they
would suffer the same fate as the Soviet Union met when confronting the mujahideen in Afghanistan—"military defeat, political
break-up, ideological downfall, and economic bankruptcy."

George W. Bush. President Bush explained the War on Terror
and the September 11 attacks in moral and patriotic terms, por-

traying the events as a demonstration of evil versus good—good being represented by America. This was first clearly articulated in a powerful speech made to a joint session of Congress on September 20, 2001. President Bush asked the question that he claimed many Americans were asking:

> "Why do they hate us?" They hate what we see right here in this chamber—a democratically elected government. . . . They hate our freedoms—our freedom of religion, our freedom of speech, our freedom to vote and assemble and disagree with each other.

He went on to equate his War on Terror with the war against "all the murderous ideologies of the twentieth century," meaning especially fascism and communism, yet he assured Congress of certain victory, because even as "freedom and fear, justice and cruelty, have always been at war . . . we know that God is not neutral between them." Furthermore, Americans also enjoyed the support of the free world: "This is the world's fight. This is civilization's fight. This is the fight of all who believe in progress and pluralism, tolerance and freedom."

The next major speech that the president gave was his "State of the Union" address on January 30, 2002. By then, the U.S. had invaded Afghanistan and was attempting to occupy and pacify it. President Bush described the war in idealistic war terms, saying that it had "saved a people from starvation" and "freed a country from brutal oppression," and that it was liberating women. Consequently, those Americans who died during the invasion "gave their lives for freedom," up against "hatred" and "madness." Nonetheless, he insisted that the War on Terror was only just beginning: history still called on America to "fight freedom's fight" against an "axis of evil," an alliance of states that support terror and are developing "weapons of mass destruction"—North Korea, Iraq and Iran. This would necessitate large defense budgets, the reorganization of "homeland security" structures at borders, popular involvement in emergency civil defense and alliances against terror with tolerant peoples around the world. The tenor of the speech was rounded off with an emphasis on the struggle for liberty: "We have known freedom's price. We have shown freedom's power. And in this great conflict, my fellow Americans, we will see freedom's victory. Thank you, and God bless."

CHRISTIANS AND THE WAR ON TERROR

Debates about how Christians should or did respond to the War on Terror were made more pressing by the coincidence that the White House and 10 Downing Street were occupied by men seen as having more religious faith than any previous incumbents for many years. In the more secular British context, Tony Blair has rarely spoken publicly about his faith, but he is known to have been influenced by Christian thinkers, be a regular churchgoer and have been a member of the Labor Party's Christian Socialist Movement. In America the politicized evangelical right has been a major element of Bush's support base. The president liked to open cabinet meetings with prayer. His Jewish adviser and admirer, David Frum, wrote in his memoirs that while White House Bible studies were not compulsory, they were "not uncompulsory" either!

This has led to much speculation and comment about the role of religion in both men's advocacy of the War on Terror in such strong moral terms. In 2006, Tony Blair told U.K. television talk-show host Michael Parkinson that he had examined his conscience before God and was ready to face his Maker for judgment on the issue of the invasion of Iraq. President Bush has frequently used religious and Christian language in talking about the War on Terror. He prayed for the airmen who launched the first strikes on Iraq in March 2003 as they tried, unsuccessfully, to kill Iraqi president Saddam Hussein and his children. On the first anniversary of the September 2001 attacks, President Bush said that the "ideal of America is the hope of all mankind. . . . That hope still shines in the darkness, and the darkness has not overcome it"—a straight quotation from John's Gospel, but here applied to America and its role in the world, rather than "the Word." Such language and theology has been sharply criticized by opponents but praised by supporters. Nonetheless, it brings into focus the question of how Christians should respond to the War on Terror.

CHRISTIAN RESPONSES TO THE WAR ON TERROR

Historically, it is possible to identify three main Christian schools of thought about war—"holy war," "just war" and "pacifism." Christian responses to the War on Terror have generally fallen into the last two categories.

Holy war sees a war as being fought upon God's orders for God's purposes and with God's assistance. Old Testament books such as Joshua are commonly cited as biblical support for this position. The crusades are the most infamous example of this category, which largely died out after World War I when the folly of all sides claiming to fight a "holy war" for Christ was starkly demonstrated. Modern mainstream Christian theologians reject holy war as unbiblical, because God's holy nation now is not the ancient people of Israel but the church. U.S. general and evangelical Christian William Boykin generated controversy in 2003 by claiming that the War on Terror was America as a "Christian nation" with a "Christian army" battling "Satan," whose forces would only be defeated militarily if "we come against them in the name of Jesus." However, this version of holy-war theology was shown to be marginal, receiving condemnation by wide sections of the American church and by President Bush distancing himself from the remarks.

Just-war theory is a tradition of moral reflection on war that considers war to be a regrettable necessity to maintain justice and limit evil in a fallen world. It considers that, under certain conditions, a Christian may, without sin, kill in war. It has pre-Christian origins in classical pagan philosophy but was adopted and adapted by Christian thinkers from the fourth century onward. It has long been the main reference point for thinking about war in the Roman Catholic Church, but Protestant thinkers (especially, in the British context, Anglicans) have also frequently turned to it. It posits a number of criteria by which the justness of a war can be judged, stipulating when a war can justly begin and how a war can be justly fought. Just-war reasoning was heavily discussed in the run up to the 2003 United States/United Kingdom invasion of Iraq, although different thinkers reached different conclusions. The pope and the archbishop of Canterbury argued that the criteria for a just war were not fulfilled, while American Catholic philosopher Jean Bethke Elshtain concluded that they were (see Study Guide 3).

Christian pacifism regards killing one's enemies as always contrary to God's will, and thereby forbids Christians from taking part in or advocating war. It relies heavily on New Testament ethical teaching, reading the commands of Christ and the apostles not to harm one's enemies as literally applicable to international conflict, not just the sphere of private relations. Evangelical pacifists (for example, the Mennonites) have also rooted it theologically in the doctrines of salvation by grace. Pacifism was the norm for the early church until the fourth century, when formerly persecuted Christians then found themselves in positions of influence with state power. Even though just-war theory subsequently displaced it as the dominant approach, it has always existed in Catholic (and later

Protestant) churches, and it has often been more popular among laypeople than theologians. In the War on Terror, evangelical leader Jim Wallis has been the most high-profile advocate of this approach, although he would not use the word *pacifist* about himself (see Study Guide 3).

Although I find the word problematic, I consider that the weight of biblical evidence provides more support for Christian pacifism than for either holy war or just-war theory (see Study Guide 3). However, discussion of these traditions of Christian reflection on warfare is not the purpose of this book. Nor am I advancing a particular understanding of the War on Terror, or advocating a certain position that Christians should adopt toward governments, protest movements or terrorist groups in their countries. The questions raised by the War on Terror are among the most important of our age, but their consideration should be rooted in a life of daily Christian worship that is fed by reflection on holy Scripture.

To that end the next chapter starts with the radical and challenging teachings of Jesus as presented in the most lengthy single body of his teaching preserved for us, the Sermon on the Mount.

PART 2

WAR AND PEACE

3

"Love Your Enemies"—
Even After September 11?

Please read Matthew 5:9, 38-48.

I once attended a wedding where the father of the bride, who had flown in from Australia, told us in his speech that he had had to get up at an "unchristian" hour to catch his plane. It struck me as a rather strange notion of what Christianity was. It reminded me of the famous faux pas by Warren Austin, U.S. delegate to the United Nations, who once offered a solution to the Arab-Israeli problem by suggesting that the Arabs and the Jews "should settle this problem in true Christian spirit"! Both of these examples typify a popular idea of what Christianity is—civilized, reasonable and, above all, "nice." This passage of Scripture from the Sermon on the Mount captures the essence of this sentiment perhaps better than any other: "Blessed are the peacemakers," "turn the other cheek," and "love your enemy." These exhortations of Christ seem to be the sort of things that it would be impossible to disagree with—what nice people do in a nice world.

But when we come to the War on Terror, is Christ's teaching genuinely useful? Take the September 11 attacks. Would we dare urge someone to "turn the other cheek" when she had heard her loved one scream through a cell phone as hijackers slit the throats of flight attendants in front of little children to gain access to cockpits, and then crashed passenger planes into skyscrapers? When we recall the nightmare scene of people choosing death by throwing themselves down from their office windows in preference to being crushed in the collapsing Twin Towers of the doomed World Trade Center, does "love your enemies" sound like anything but an obscenity? Such exhortations seem to overlook the horror of that terrible day and deny the instinct for retaliation or protection of self and others. That principle catapulted singer Toby Keith to the top of the charts with his song "The Angry American." Endorsing the U.S. attack on Afghanistan in October 2001, it boasted to the Taliban/bin Laden/Afghanis that "we lit up your sky" like an Independence Day firework celebration, telling them they would be sorry that they messed with America, who would "put a boot in your a**" in the American way.

However, it is not only such American reactions that call into question the relevance of Jesus' teaching. Popular responses to 9/11 in the Muslim world are also revealing. In Palestine some people celebrated in the streets. A friend showed me a text message from an Uzbekistani: "Did you see what happened? Tee hee hee hee hee! . . . I am so glad." Why? In his speeches, Osama bin Laden frequently referred to Palestine and Iraq. Britain helped create the state of Israel after it conquered Palestine, and the United States has been its staunchest backer politically, financially and militarily. Britain has enabled Israel to build a large nuclear arsenal, yet America has shielded it from the United Nations' demands over forty years to exit all Palestinian territories that it occupies. On the other hand, the U.S. and U.K. used the United Nations to evict Iraq from Kuwait in a matter of months in 1990 and 1991 when that suited our interests. Throughout the 1990s we continued to wage a low-level war of bombing and sanctions that led to the deaths of hundreds of thousands of children. In 1998 Denis Halliday resigned as the UN aid coordinator for Iraq in protest, saying: "We are in the process of destroying an entire society. It is as simple and terrifying as that. It is illegal and immoral." In 2003 the U.S. and the U.K. invaded Iraq, allegedly to disarm it of "weapons of mass destruction," and tens of thousands of people have been killed in the bloodshed that has unfolded. Wherever I have traveled in the Muslim world, I have encountered anger at these perceived double standards.

I was staying in a back-street guesthouse in the ancient Uzbekistani city of Bukhara in November of 2004, as U.S. marines attacked the Iraqi city of Falluja. Untold numbers of civilians and insurgents died as fighting destroyed much of the city. In the course of our conversations, I mentioned to the good-humored and genteel hotel owner that I was a Christian, and quoted to him from the passage in Matthew from the beginning of this chapter. He immediately exploded in anger. Pointing to relayed CNN television footage of corpses littering Falluja's streets, he shouted at me, "Don't talk to me about Christians! Who is slaughtering all those wretched Iraqis at the moment? Christians!" Could we dare look these victims and their families or sympathizers in the eye and say "love us, do good to us, pray for us and seek our best"?

So, far from being reasonable and noble, it would seem that these words of Jesus from the Sermon on the Mount are quite the opposite: unnatural, unrealistic and unworkable. Do they have *any* relevance to the real world and to Christians from Britain, Iraq, America, Palestine and elsewhere, as we find ourselves caught up in the War on Terror? I believe that in these words of Jesus we see a remarkable description of God's character, and a call to discipleship that offers the greatest hope both for our own lives and for our suffering world. They help us to understand the War on Terror and guide our responses to it. In particular, Matthew 5:38-48 summarizes perfectly *what* Jesus said we should do to our enemies, *why* we should do it and *how* he put it into practice.

WHAT SHOULD WE DO TO OUR ENEMIES?

Over the centuries, few of Jesus' teachings have been debated as intensely as his commands to love our enemies. Does it *really* mean we must not harm them in any way, even if they are underground terrorists trying to blow up our workplaces, or enlisted soldiers trying to bomb our cities? D. A. Carson, in his book *Love in Hard Places*, tackles this in relation to the War on Terror.[1] He argues that Jesus was not meant to be understood absolutely but was reacting against tendencies of his day, such as petty personal vindictiveness. It is thus "important not to infer too much" from this passage, he says, and he takes it to inform such conduct as treating prisoners well. He also argues that far from Jesus' commands ruling out war, they may actually require it, as loving enemies may mean having to invade them to help them in the long run, for example by overthrowing a tyrannical ruler. Thus, he states, "war can be a form of love."

Oswald Chambers, the Bible teacher and pastor whose writings have challenged generations of Christians to an intense and uncompromising daily spiritual walk with Christ, said, "If you dispute the Sermon on the Mount with your head, you will blunt the appeal to your heart." Likewise, the Danish philosopher Søren Kierkegaard once said that Christianity is not difficult to understand: "love your enemies" is so simple that even a child can understand it. No, what is difficult is to put it into practice, he said, and therefore advised avoiding commentaries by theologians trying to explain why Jesus did not mean what he said. "Christian scholarship," he wrote, "is the Church's invention to defend itself against the Bible." The Bible is not a set of ideas to be debated and dismissed at will but, in the classic formula of the Westminster Confession, is given by God to reveal "all things necessary for His own glory, man's salvation, faith and life." Countless Christians down through the ages have testified that the Scriptures are a "lamp to [our] feet / and a light for [our] path[s]" (Psalm 119:105) as we walk through life with Christ.

No, we are told to love our enemies, seek *their* good, ask what *their* interests are, pray that God would bless *them*. Could it be that simple? What would happen if, instead of trying to explain away Jesus' very uncomfortable teaching on loving our enemies, or using it to back up a nicely worked-out theological position, we dared to take it seriously and live it out as we face deadly enemies in the War on Terror?

WHY DID JESUS TELL US TO LOVE OUR ENEMIES?

Jesus told us to love our enemies. But why? Was it because that is what reasonable people do, and that by being nice we will be able to win over as friends those with whom we have fallen out? That is how our conflict-averse culture thinks. Even a cursory reading of the Gospel accounts of Christ's arguments with the scribes and Pharisees shows that this was neither how Jesus taught nor lived. Why, then, did Jesus tell us to love our enemies? The answer is simply because it is in the very nature of God to do so, and Jesus commands us to be like him: "Be perfect . . . as your heavenly Father is perfect" (verse 48), "that you may be children of your Father in heaven" (verse 45 TNIV). What does this Father do? He is good to all, however undeserving: "He causes his sun to rise on the evil and the good, and sends rain on the righteous and the unrighteous" (verse 45). The "unrighteous" surely includes everyone! Jesus used most of the Sermon on the Mount up until these verses to disabuse his listeners, and us, of the idea that by ourselves we are good enough for God. We think that we are able to judge others, that because we have not killed anyone, we are more holy and deserving of God's favor than terrorists like Osama bin Laden. But in Matthew 5:21-24, Jesus pointedly shows us that if we have even secretly been angry with another human being without reason and hated them, we are in danger of the very same judgment as the murderer. "For whoever keeps the whole law and yet stumbles at just one point is guilty of breaking all of it," writes James (2:10); and Paul declares that "all have sinned and fall short of the glory of God" (Romans 3:23).

Until we grasp this biblical view of ourselves as sinners, we will be unable to understand why Jesus teaches us to love our enemies and be peacemakers, and why that is what makes us children of God. We like to think that we are generally good people. But the Bible teaches us that "all our righteous acts are like filthy rags" before God (Isaiah 64:6). As individuals and a race, we have continually rebelled against our holy and just Maker, who created us to be like him. But, as Paul declares in utter amazement in Romans 5:8, "God demonstrates his own love for us in this: While we were still sinners [or 'enemies' as he says in verse 10], Christ died for us." It is simply God's grace that justifies us, making us his children and giving us eternal life. That is why we are to love our enemies—to imitate the boundless love of God for us by loving our enemies in the same way.

HOW DID JESUS LOVE HIS ENEMIES?

Christ commanded us to love our enemies because God loved us, his enemies. But Jesus was not just giving us lofty, moral ideals; he fulfilled them perfectly in his own life. He lived under the shadow of political violence from the moment that he was born. Herod tried to kill him by massacring all newborn babies, and Jesus would have grown up with bitter communal memory of this outrage. But this was merely the tip of the iceberg; a vicious cycle of taxation and violent repression by occupying Rome and its corrupt puppet rulers intensified with each uprising by the desperate Jewish people. Jesus thus began his public ministry in highly charged revolutionary times. People were looking for a military savior to free them from the Romans. As the one claiming to be the long-sought messiah, everything he said and did was intensely political.

Jesus was continually tempted with the option of misusing power and violence to save his people. That was the temptation Satan offered him in the wilderness: "all the kingdoms of the world" if he would bow down and worship (Luke 4:5). On more than one occasion, Christ resisted being crowned as king by the crowds. In chapter 13 of his Gospel, Luke recounts how people came to Jesus to break the news of a terrible atrocity committed by government forces against civilians. They were no doubt excited: this would surely be an ideal moment for this would-be king to stir up the people in rebellion. After all, in the previous chapter he had declared that he had come to "bring fire on the earth" (Luke 12:49). However, refusing to ride any wave of popular outrage, Christ instead warned them to look at their own sin. Later, he called Peter "Satan" for trying to prevent him from going to his death, shattering Peter's vision of a glorious military overthrow of the Romans. As he entered Jerusalem, Jesus wept that its inhabitants did not know what would bring them peace, prophesying that the Jews would not love their enemies but hate and fight them, thereby missing the kingdom of God and bringing ruin upon their own city (Luke 19:41-44).

As well as warning his followers not to hate their foes, Christ also demonstrated love to the enemies of his people. He befriended collaborating traitors like tax collectors, made despised Samaritans the heroes of his stories and even praised the faith of an occupying Roman soldier. When soldiers came to arrest Jesus, Peter took out his sword and struck one of those who had come to seize his master. But Jesus *healed* his enemy, warning his followers that "all who draw the sword will die by the sword" (Matthew 26:52). He practiced what he preached, showing us that our enemies are to be overcome through love not hatred, demonstrating that God's kingdom was not to be established in the ways that human kingdoms are.

This demonstration of enemy love took him finally to the cross. Theologian Miroslav Volf, writing from the experience of his native Croatia being overrun by its enemies and engulfed in a war of tit-for-tat massacres, said that by his death Jesus "broke the cycle of violence."[2] As the sinless one, he was the only person ever completely justified in striking back. However, he did not, but instead hung on the cross, loving his enemies and praying "Father, forgive them." His was the ultimate example of enemy love.

Jesus called God, "my Father," and tells us that if we love our enemies and become peacemakers, we too will become "children of God." Who wouldn't want to be that? As Jürgen Moltmann said, "It sounds like Christmas everywhere!"[3] But Jesus called God "my Father" and left home and family, was ridiculed, was considered unpatriotic, and in the end was executed in agony as a criminal. Jesus did this for us, his enemies. There is nothing "natural" about this. It is supernatural love that reached out, sought, disarmed and wooed us when we were his enemies. As his Spirit lives in us, we discover the tremendous power of that same love, and are liberated to love our enemies in ways that we previously thought of as unnatural or unrealistic. Paul calls this the "gospel [good news] of peace" (Ephesians 6:15). It is good news indeed: good news for sinners in need of a savior, and good news for a world of suicide bombers and superpowers trapped in a cycle of self-righteous violence.

LOVING OUR ENEMIES IN THE WAR ON TERROR

In the mid third century, the Christians in the North African city of Carthage had been subjected to a ten-month period of persecution, where they chose not to use violence to defend themselves. This was followed by a deadly outbreak of disease. Many people fled, but Bishop Cyprian preached a sermon where he said "there is nothing remarkable in cherishing merely our own people. . . . We should do something more than heathens, overcoming evil with good, and practicing merciful kindness like that of God, we should love our enemies as well." The Christians remained in the city, feeding and tending their suffering persecutors. This led to great growth in the church. In his assessment of how Christianity spread so rapidly in the early church, historian Robin Lane Fox said that it proclaimed an attractive message that spoke to the weak points of Roman culture.[4] One of those he identified as violence—in a time when war and violence were seen as the norm, and even celebrated, the Christian gospel of peacemaking was immensely attractive.

To the extent that war remains a normal part of our culture and even daily experience, modern Christians find themselves in a similar position. British and American Christians both live in a two-party political consensus that insists that the War on Terror is the correct response to Islamist terrorism. Palestinian and Iraqi Christians likewise inhabit a culture where violent resistance to Israeli and British/American occupiers is seen by many as necessary and noble. Are we willing to subject all of these forms of political common sense to the wisdom of the Bible, and then dare to live out in faith the teachings of Jesus in our world? This will not be easy, but that should hardly be surprising. We may not protest that these are exceptional times, or that everything has changed. The idea that we can ignore what Jesus taught us if we think that our enemies are *really* evil is a denial that Christianity works in the real world. "The Christian ideal has not been tried and found wanting," said G. K. Chesterton. "It has been found difficult, and left untried."

"Love your enemies" was no doubt an uncomfortable, indeed an incredible, challenge to Jesus' hearers, suffering as they were under the terror of occupation. Two millennia have done nothing to rob it of its power to disturb us and cut through our commonsense political and theological understandings of the world. The Jesus who loved us as his enemies and gave his life for us calls us all to turn from our sin. He freely invites us to walk from death into life, to enter his kingdom and become children of God. We do that by loving *our* enemies, by copying the God who abundantly pours out his goodness on the righteous and the unrighteous alike.

Because it is at the heart of the gospel message of justification by faith, Christ's instruction to love our enemies is also one of great evangelical hope. We have no reason to be confused each time a war happens; far from it, we have a marvelous message to proclaim to an aching world, a message of God's abundant, overwhelming and undeserved love that reconciles people to God and to each other. Far from being unrealistic and unreasonable, the Bible's command to "love your enemies" is precisely the message that all sides in the War on Terror need to hear and, more importantly, need to do.

4

Why Does God Allow War and Terrorism?

Please read Jeremiah 4:11-27.

We saw in the previous chapter that Jesus commands us to love our enemies. But that only begs the question: why do we have enemies in the first place? Why does God allow war and terrorism? This is one of the questions that Christians are often asked, and indeed often ask themselves, when their people or country is subject to bloody and violent attack. If God is indeed both good and "Almighty," then why could he not simply intervene on behalf of innocent lives to prevent the September 11 hijackers from perpetrating their dastardly attack, and stop men like Saddam Hussein and George W. Bush going to war with each other?

This question is neither asked nor answered directly in Scripture. However, it is implicitly addressed in many places, and this passage from Jeremiah is one of the most poignant. Indeed, it is one of the darkest moments of the Bible's darkest book: Jeremiah is all about war. The historical context is the invasions of Judah by the Babylonians around the turn of the sixth century B.C. In this passage, Jeremiah announces a terrifying prophetic vision of the appalling destruction that enemy armies will wreak on the land in the future. While we must be careful not to remove the passage from its context, the book of Jeremiah seems eerily relevant to us today. We only need to read the newspapers to realize that Jeremiah's signature cry of "terror on every side" could well be a description of our age. In verse 27 of this passage, the prophet announces God declaring, "The whole land will be ruined, / though I will not destroy it completely." This verse illuminates the whole section and enables us to see how Jeremiah makes sense of his time, and it throws light on God's purpose in allowing war down through the ages.

WAR—THE UNDOING OF GOD'S CREATION

"The whole land will be ruined." This awful chapter speaks of the terrible reality of war as the utter contradiction of God's will and plan for humanity. Verses 23-26 are a shocking fourfold study of God's work of Genesis 1 and 2 undone. Where God initially looked at his creation and "saw that it was good," in these verses we see that his prophet looked four times, but found the opposite.

First, in verse 23 Jeremiah looks and sees the earth "formless and empty," exactly the description of Genesis 1:1 before God began creation. This is God's good creation work cancelled out, reversed even. Where God had said "let there be light," he sees only darkness. One commentator suggested this was due to the abundance of smoke and fire from the burning cities, which reminds us of the blazing fires of Kuwait following the 1990-1991 Gulf War.

Next, in verse 24 the prophet looks and sees the mountains quaking. Elie Wiesel, the Holocaust survivor, said he understood this verse only when he learned of Babi Yar in the Ukraine, where Germans killed 80,000 Jews during World War II, and the weight of decomposing corpses piled in a ravine literally made the mountains quake.[1]

Third, in verse 25 the prophet looks yet sees no people. God had expressly instructed Eve and Adam to "go forth and multiply," yet Jeremiah foresaw a time when his people had been killed, deported or had fled to Egypt. We can picture this by recalling the harrowing images of Iraqis fleeing the American bombardments of Falluja in 2004, and mangled corpses piling up in its emptying streets. Furthermore, although God filled the earth with teeming life, verse 25 tells us that even the birds had flown away. Auschwitz survivors remembered that bird song was not heard over the camp as they fled the noxious tempest of the incinerator fires.

Finally, in verse 26 Jeremiah looks and sees the once fruitful land as a desert, and the formerly thriving cities desolate. We may think of the destruction of the Twin Towers in New York, or verdant cities like Kabul in Afghanistan and Grozny in Chechnya devastated by the colossal violence of recent conflicts when powerful states have bombarded weak ones. War is the undoing of God's life-giving creation, the negation of his good work.

If, therefore, war is such a bad thing and so contrary to his will for the earth as revealed in creation, why does a good God allow it to happen? This question may be asked both by opponents of religion and by believers genuinely trying to make sense of a violent world. Insofar as the question acknowledges that war is an evil, that it is not how God intended us to live, it is a good question. But in so far as it blames God, it is the wrong one. What answer does this passage give? One word, in verse 17—"rebelled"! Rebellion against God's righteous decrees, or sin, was at the root of Judah's trouble in Jeremiah's day, and is the root of all ours today. As we saw in the previous chapter, Martyn Lloyd-Jones, the great preacher at Westminster Chapel, London, addressed this very question.[2] He said, "The Bible does not isolate war as something unique—no, it is one manifestation of sin, and one of its consequences." We see this in verse 18, where the prophet unequivocally thunders: "Your own conduct and actions / have brought this upon you." If the human race obeyed the Ten Commandments, if we lived according to the way Christ instructed us in the Sermon on the Mount, there would be no war, no invasions, no terrorism. We cannot blame God—human sin has brought it upon us.

GOD'S SPARING GRACE

If Jeremiah had closed his message on that note, we could have no grounds for complaint of injustice on God's part. But it does not end there! No, in the second part of verse 27, God says, "I will not destroy it completely." What does he mean? God has spared the human race, not allowing it to suffer all the consequences of its rebellion. God has spared our country, not visiting upon us all the iniquity and violence that we have visited upon others. God has spared us as individuals, as we have been saved from suffering the full consequences of our sin. Why? Because of one thing and one thing only, his great mercy—as the Bible says, he does not "[want] anyone to perish, but everyone to come to repentance" (2 Peter 3:9). Augustine famously said that God made us for himself, and our hearts are restless until they find their rest in him. But to read the prophets is to read of God as a brokenhearted lover who longs for his wayward bride to return to him, that he might shower his love upon her again. It is to read of a God who made us for himself and whose *own* heart is restless until we find our rest in him.

This theme of salvation is like a golden thread running through this dark book. Jeremiah had glimpses of a new age that Jehovah would usher in, when his people again would be saved. In chapter 3 he spoke of a time when the people would forget the ark of the covenant of the Lord. Was this blasphemy? No, they would dwell under a new covenant, when all nations would gather to honor the Lord—a world of peace and compassion and justice. In glimpsing the initiator of this new covenant, a king, "The LORD our Righteousness" (Jeremiah 23:6), Jeremiah foresaw Christ, whose death and resurrection would reunite a rebellious race to God. The reality of this new covenant is demonstrated wherever Christ's kingdom reign of peace, justice and righteousness is faithfully proclaimed and lived out in our lives, and it will finally be consummated at his second coming.

So, what are we to do in the meantime? What did Jeremiah do? We hear him pour out his inner feelings in verses 19-20, "Oh, my anguish, my anguish! / I writhe in pain." His anguish at the terrible consequences of war and terror drove him to cry out ceaselessly to God in prayer, and to take the lonely and unpopular road of calling his generation to repentance from their rebellion and plans for war. He did not simply take comfort in the promise of future salvation, nor did he sit back smugly and say "I told you so!" when disaster struck. Nor is this some sort of small-minded nationalism that hopes his side will win a war—later in the book we see him mourning and lamenting over the violence that will befall "enemy" nations. No, Jeremiah was called by God, as we are, to be loyal to a greater kingdom, a greater vision. This has always been the burden of God's servants down through the ages, and it should be ours today.

HENRY MARTYN

One instructive example of how to respond and to negotiate the competing loyalties to the kingdom of God and our warring countries is provided by Henry Martyn.[3] A brilliant Cambridge undergraduate who was the university's top student in both Latin and mathematics at the beginning of the nineteenth century, Henry Martyn abandoned a promising academic career to train for ordained ministry. After serving as curate under Charles Simeon at Holy Trinity Church in Cambridge, he became the first Anglican graduate missionary to India. He dedicated his life to founding schools, preaching to the indigenous populations, and making Hindi and Farsi translations of Scripture. On hearing of the death of his sister from the hereditary tuberculosis from which he too suffered, he wrote in his diary: "now let me burn out for God." That is indeed what he did, eventually dying in Turkey on his way home to marry his beloved Lydia.

The diary and letters of Henry Martyn are often read as an inspiration for fervent devotion and uncompromising and costly commitment to Christ.[4] However, they also provide rich lessons for living out that commitment when our country is at war. He lived during the Napoleonic Wars, a period of great international upheaval as the British Empire clashed with its European rivals in a struggle from which it emerged as a world superpower. The nation grew fabulously wealthy through a combination of force, trade, investment and imperial ideology. Inspired by a classical education, the British saw themselves as the heirs to the civilizing legacy of ancient Rome, spreading education, trade and good governance. The arrogant belief that God had entrusted them with this task is reflected in the words of A. C. Benson's well-known national hymn, "Land of Hope and Glory":

> Wider still and wider, shall thy bounds be set;
> God, who made thee mighty, make thee mightier yet.

Many commentators today draw parallels between the Britain of the nineteenth century and the United States of the twenty-first. With the demise of the Soviet Union, America stands as the sole superpower. Like Britain before it, the idea of having a "manifest destiny" to spread civilization across the globe lies at the core of its founding beliefs. America now sees itself as the world's moral policeman, fighting the War on Terror on behalf of humanity. Martyn wrestled with the question of how a believer should act as a citizen of such a military state but also remain true to the Lord, and his example is instructive to us.

The Battle of Blaauwberg and the "War of the Lamb." Sailing out on an East India Company vessel to begin missionary work in India in 1806, Martyn became embroiled in the Battle of Blaauwberg off South Africa's Cape of Good Hope. In January 1806, a fleet of sixty-one British ships dropped anchor at Robben Island and landed 6,000 troops, who captured Cape Town in a short battle. As Martyn's biographer, Richard France, wrote: "It was his only taste of war, and it revolted him." Martyn, who attended to the dead and dying on the battlefield, recorded his vivid observations in his diary and in a long letter back to Simeon in Cambridge.

Martyn saw in warfare the ugly reality of sin and humanity's need for the gospel. Touring a makeshift hospital and seeing some two hundred casualties, he recorded that "a more ghastly spectacle than that which presented itself here I could not have conceived." He "shuddered at considering what a multitude of souls must be passing into eternity." Martyn took no pleasure in the capture of Cape Town, even though it was a significant stage in the consolidation of Britain's empire. Indeed, on seeing the British flag newly flying over the Dutch fort, he wrote: "I felt considerable pain at the enemy's being obliged to give up their fort and town. . . . I hate the cruel pride and arrogance that makes men boast over a conquered foe." Rather, he sought the glory of the kingdom of God. He told Simeon that he "prayed that the capture of the Cape might be ordered to the advancement of Christ's kingdom," and that England "might show herself great indeed, by sending forth ministers of her church to diffuse the gospel of peace." He expressed in his journal the desire to "carry the war into the enemy's territory," but for Martyn, as for Paul, his weapons were "not carnal, but mighty through God to the pulling down of strongholds." Thus he dedicated his life to the translation and preaching of the gospel.

Henry Martyn sorrowed over war, seeing it as a product and demonstration of sin, which should spur the Christian on to pray and work for the gospel. On witnessing the casualties at Blaauw-berg, he wrote that these scenes made him yearn for that day "when nation shall not lift up sword against nation," and redouble his resolution to hasten its coming: "may the remembrance of this day ever excite me to pray and labour more for the propagation of the gospel of peace." Christians would do well even today to share the same radical resolve.

PART 3

CITIZENS OF HEAVEN

Living with Two Passports

Please read Philippians 3:12-21 and Jeremiah 29:1-23.

In the second part of this book we looked at the "big issues" of war, terrorism and salvation. In this third part, we explore in more detail some practical aspects of how we can make sense of and respond to war. What this means in practice is that we need to think through the tensions of being both citizens of heaven and citizens of an earthly state.

"Citizenship," or belonging to a certain country and holding its passport, is one of the most sensitive political topics of our time. Should we allow more noncitizens to migrate into our countries to work? Should we give citizenship to those already here? Should we oblige people to perform the responsibilities of citizenship, for example, by making them vote? Is it right that less well-off citizens of the same country generally enjoy poorer health and lower educational attainments than richer ones? Should we demand that schoolchildren have "citizenship" classes to learn the cultural values of their country and, if so, what exactly are those values? It is little wonder that citizenship is often one of the fiercest political battlegrounds in modern states.

Our citizenship is one of the most important things about us. It tells a story about who we are and where we come from. It also goes a long way toward determining our life chances. If we have the citizenship of certain countries, we can expect to live well over seventy years, and have access to free health care and education. Children born with some other citizenship may consider themselves fortunate to reach forty, and have little access to health care, education and other social services. If we happen to be born with the citizenship of a rich country, we may be able to pass freely and easily over borders around the world. If we begin life with some other citizenship, we may end up as one of the hundreds of drowned would-be migrants washed up on Europe's shores each year, or parched to death in Arizona's desert trying to cross the border from Mexico, hoping to enter to get "a slice of the cake." It is little wonder that modern citizenship has been compared by some writers to medieval inherited feudal privilege.

Citizenship is not only about privilege, but allegiance. When millions of people scream and cheer in front of the television at eleven young men whom they have never met, just because they kick a soccer ball past a similar group of men whom they also have not met, it demonstrates just how significant citizenship is. When those same millions cheer on armies of such young men as they slaughter others similarly unknown to them in battle, we are reminded how fearfully important citizenship is. In our world, we cannot escape citizenship.

WHAT DOES PAUL MEAN BY CITIZENSHIP?

Just as we cannot ignore the importance of citizenship in the modern world, neither can we escape it in the Bible, as these passages from Philippians and Jeremiah remind us. Following the destruction of the Jewish states by the Babylonians, the cream of the Israelite population was deported to exile in Babylon. In this passage from Jeremiah, we see the letter he wrote informing them that God would deliver them in his own good time. In the meantime, however, he urged them to throw themselves into the life of the place of their sojourn, to seek its peace and prosperity without losing sight of their ultimate allegiance to God. As New Testament writers conceive of Christians as exiles, strangers and pilgrims on the earth (1 Peter 1:1; Hebrews 11:13), this letter has been read by the church as providing an attractive ethic of negotiating competing citizenships.

Paul takes up this theme in his letters. In Philippians 3:20, he writes, "our citizenship is in heaven." It would be a mistake to read into this statement the complex significance of the twenty-first-century nation-state. But citizenship meant a great deal to the people of Philippi, to whom this letter is addressed. Their town was a Roman colony, founded by people granted Roman citizenship. They had been rewarded for military service or generosity to the state by being included in it, and citizenship was an honor that was respected and desired. A central register was kept listing all citizens in the town, those who had the special rights and privileges of belonging.

It is striking how the most important aspects of belonging to earthly nations are applied to the church in the New Testament. According to Peter, the church is a "holy nation": the word he uses is *ethnos*, which we would more commonly render today as "ethnic group" (1 Peter 2:9). Christians are "citizens" of another country, a heavenly "homeland" (see Hebrews 11:14-16). They are "Christ's ambassadors" (2 Corinthians 5:20), foreigners in the land where they are living, whose work is loyally to pursue the interests of their home country. They have different laws and codes of conduct under which they live. Perhaps supremely, they have an ultimate allegiance not to Caesar as head of state, but to King Jesus. No wonder that the early anti-Christian philosopher, Celsius, condemned the church as politically subversive precisely because of this.

Of course, the church was not meant to take over the earthly nations and states and their functions. These are often presented in a negative light in the New Testament, which generally paints a very sorry picture of the exercise of Jewish and Roman justice and power (for example, the trial and crucifixion of Jesus). The New Testament writers were under no illusions about their moral nature (Colossians 2:15). This being so, Christians are still to respect the governing authorities (1 Peter 2:17), as they play a God-ordained role in maintaining order by promoting virtue and countering vice (Romans 12:17—13:7), a role different from that of the church. Nonetheless, the Christian's primary identity and allegiance were as a citizen of heaven, not Israel, Rome or anywhere else.

Celsius was thus only partially right about the subversion of the church. This was a very different kind of kingdom. The citizens of this kingdom share their wealth freely with those in want, sure that their king will provide all they need. They do not jealously protect their borders, but welcome all who will to freely take citizenship. They do not hate their enemies—not only do they refuse to harm them, but they love and pray for their good. They do not joyfully line up behind their tribes when they go to war, but sorrow over violence and injustice, and actively seek to be peacemakers. In a world torn apart by misconceived notions of citizenship, they are exactly the kind of kingdom citizens that we need more of, as "salt and light" (Matthew 5:13-14) in global society.

CITIZENS OF HEAVEN TODAY

The notion of Christians as citizens of heaven, who seek the peace and prosperity of the places they happen to pass through on earth, is an appealing one. However, as history shows, reality does not always match that ideal. As one commentator wryly put it, Jesus commanded us to love our enemies, although one would never have guessed as much from the conduct of his followers! In his autobiography, the U.K.'s former lord chancellor, the late Lord Hailsham, sardonically wrote of the church that "the civil wars . . . the pogroms, the crusades, the sackings, the holy wars, are not, one would think, good advertisements for the divine society, inspired by the Holy Spirit, against whom we are expressly told the gates of hell shall not prevail."[1]

That ambiguous history is illustrated by the place where I did my graduate studies and later worked as a researcher, Sidney Sussex College in Cambridge. Above the inner entrance to the college chapel is a statue of England's patron saint, St. George: the archetypal armed Christian warrior in armor with the cross on his shield, killing for God's cause and his country. It symbolizes what happens when we get our citizenships mixed up and, sadly, is the story of so much of church history. But at the other end of the chapel stands a statue of St. Francis. He was converted from his earlier days as a "godly" warrior on the crusades when he heard God's voice challenging him, "You have misunderstood the vision. It will have a different fulfillment." He went on to found an order of monks that were to work for the peace of Christ by refusing to bear arms. He came to oppose the crusades, actually going to see Sultan Al Kamil in 1219, and to show Christ's love in acts of humble service. Apparently, the testimony of this lone man deeply impressed the sultan. Francis grasped Paul's sense of citizenship more keenly than any crusader.

What would that mean for us in our world today? Of course, different Christians may well reach different conclusions, and that is as it should be. But two examples of people who have particularly inspired me are worth considering for how they negotiated the claims of competing citizenships, those of their warring nation-states and those of the kingdom of heaven.

The first example is a network of American Christians in the
1980s.[2] The administration of President Reagan was supporting a
number of right-wing governments and paramilitary bands in Central America, (most famously the Nicaraguan Contras). These brutal groups tortured and murdered people whom they thought were
sympathetic to the poor, including trade union organizers, doctors,
teachers and church workers. Many fled Central America to the
United States, but the Reagan government deported them to its allies, where they were often murdered (soon after arrival at the air-
port). Finding their protests falling on deaf ears, U.S. churches were
faced with a dilemma: to obey their earthly government or be loyal
to the values of their heavenly kingdom. Many chose the latter, set-
ting up an underground network to smuggle people into the country and conceal them and give them sanctuary. They modeled it on
the famous nineteenth-century "underground railroad" established
to help runaway slaves to safety.

American Christians even put themselves in danger, trying to address the problems at their source. As part of the "Witness for
Peace" program, ordinary believers went out to Nicaragua and
acted as human shields to protect those people that their government regarded as enemies. They lived in villages at risk of attack,
and also trailed Contra forces with cameras and notebooks, betting
on their citizenship that the Contras would not harm citizens of the
country that was financially backing them. Some 5,000 took part,
giving up their annual holidays to do this, risking their lives, and
returning to spread the word in churches and the media about what
their government was doing. This multifaceted campaign eventually forced changes in government policy. For example, in 1988
when Congress voted down support for the Contras, church cam-
paigning pressure was stated as one reason.

This is inspiring, but perhaps one may object, "That is fine in a liberal state, but it would not work elsewhere." That is not true. Jesus said that he would build his church, and the very gates of hell—let alone some earthly power, however hellish it might seem in our eyes—would not prevail against it. One of the most remarkable episodes of World War II relates to the French village of Le Chambon and the pastor of the Protestant church there, André Trocmé.[3] He was a man with a keen sense of what citizenship in Christ's kingdom actually meant. Despising fascist brutality, he led the area where he was pastor in resisting first Vichy France and then the Nazis. But this was not by joining the armed resistance, whose methods he also considered contrary to the laws of his kingdom. Rather, moving from symbolic resistance to active organization, he helped to create an extensive system to protect and conceal Jewish refugees. Jews came to them from all over France, and indeed from occupied Europe including Germany itself. The people of Le Chambon saved the lives of hundreds, possibly thousands. Trocmé himself survived the war, including time spent in a prison camp and on the run from the Gestapo, to become an important figure in postwar Franco-German reconciliation.

THE KING IN HISTORY

The Christians in 1980s America and 1940s Le Chambon are merely two examples of people who seized the biblical truth that they were citizens of heaven before they were members of a certain nation-state, and thus transformed the world around them. There are countless more such examples, most of them unsung heroes. None were perfect, and few found it easy to swim against the tide. Their secret was not moral courage, optimism, hidden strength or any such merely human quality. No, all had one thing in common. They believed that their citizenship of the heavenly kingdom was more important than their citizenship of any earthly state, and they believed that their king would help them live out kingdom lives.

And that is the crux of the matter: the king. Although we say the word so easily, a God who is a king is a very uncomfortable thought. A God who, in the words of the Nanci Griffiths country-and-western song, lives "at a distance"? Great. A God existing in each and every human like a little-used organ, which deals with our higher moral and creative instincts? Even better. A God who is merely a "personal savior" that we can take around with us like an iPod, and turn on and off at will? Best of all. But a God who is a king, a lord, a sovereign? Now that is something else. That is a God who rules and reigns, who interrupts and interacts, who will change our lives and our worlds if we dare to accept citizenship in his kingdom, and to take that citizenship seriously. There are no quotas limiting citizenship in this kingdom: no, all are invited to enter freely, by faith in the merits of Christ alone, who died for our sins and was raised to life for our justification (Romans 4:25). To take up that passport is the beginning of a royal adventure, more real and more glorious than the drama of any great nation-state.

A Tale of Two Cities

NATIONALISM, TERRORISM AND RECONCILIATION

Please read Acts 10:1-23.

We have been considering how to live as both citizens of heaven and citizens of our countries in the War on Terror. Obviously, citizenship is connected to geography; it is about belonging to certain places. This passage from the Acts of the apostles is about two places, Caesarea and Joppa. As every geographer will tell you, places are important. We are often told that we live in an age of globalization, where Internet communications, worldwide supermarket chains, and universally recognized brands of clothing, cars, food and music are leading to a standardized world. However, from our own experience we know that that is not the case. Individual places keep their own special character, their own unique mix of local and global cultures. The very mention of the names of cities and towns that we have lived in or traveled through may trigger wonderfully happy, or intensely painful, memories.

However, as well as being highly evocative of personal experience, places can also be the focus of conflict. In football, for example, simply to say "Bears and Packers" or "Cowboys and Redskins" in the same sentence immediately reminds us of bitter rivalries and jealousies. Even to mention the name of some places can reveal a great deal about our politics. In Northern Ireland, Catholics say "Derry" and Protestants "Londonderry" for the same town, and woe to you if you use the wrong name in the wrong company! Control of Lebanon's capital city, Beirut, was bitterly contested between Christian and Muslim militias and American forces in the 1980s. But perhaps most tragic of all is Jerusalem, a holy place for many Christians, Jews and Muslims, yet one that has been fiercely fought over since being conquered by Israel in the 1967 Arab-Israeli wars.

One of the finest books ever written about places and the way that they divide us is G. K. Chesterton's novel *The Napoleon of Notting Hill*.[1] It is a story about the division of London into independent boroughs, each with its own made-up emblem, army, fabricated history and territory. The division was originally intended as something comic, to entertain the bored King Auberon. However, the plan backfires when Adam Wayne, the leader of one tinpot state, Notting Hill, takes his job deadly seriously and organizes wars against his neighbors for the honor of Notting Hill.

Chesterton was writing a satire about the problem of nationalism—when nations struggle with each other in disputes about who owns a certain place. The twentieth century was scourged by nationalism, from major conflicts like World Wars I and II to smaller but still bloody ones such as those terrorist campaigns for national independence for the Catholics of Northern Ireland, the Basque people of Spain or the Tamil people of Sri Lanka. In his analysis of suicide bombing, Robert Pape argues that most such terrorist campaigns have been waged by people trying to secure the independence of their native lands.[2] International bodies like the European Union and the United Nations were set up after World War II to try to prevent any more wars over nationalism, but it is a problem that refuses to go away. It is for this reason that Acts 10 is so fascinating and so important; it shows not only that nationalism can be overcome, but that the church was born in the act of overcoming it. Are there lessons here for our own age, torn as it is by nationalism and violence?

CAESAREA AND JOPPA—A TALE OF TWO CITIES

Good stories have good places in them, and this passage from Acts 10 is a tale of two cities, Caesarea and Joppa. Caesarea was where Cornelius the Roman centurion lived, and the apostle Peter lived in Joppa. Theologian Alan Kreider has suggested that the meaning of these places is very important. There was only thirty miles between them geographically, but culturally they were a universe apart. Joppa was very Jewish, the sort of place where good, traditional, religious Jews would live. Peter was just such a person, a devoted follower of his ancient religion, excited because he knew Jesus, the Messiah for whom his people had waited. Caesarea was totally different. It was an imperial city, a garrison town built by the Romans to help them govern and control Palestine. It was a magnificent port, with grand Roman architecture intended to display the power and wealth of the Empire and constantly remind the Jews just who ruled the place. Indeed, it was home to the local military garrison and headquarters that coordinated the occupation. It was named after the emperor, whom Romans worshiped as a living god—which was of course blasphemy for the Jews. Therefore, even the mention of the name of this city would have been a painful reminder to the Jews that they were under foreign subjugation. We are told that one of the two central characters in this passage, Cornelius, was a Roman officer of the Italian regiment, which meant that he was a native of the heart of the Empire, and thus likely to be fiercely loyal to Rome.

So these two cities were against each other, and the two people at the center of this story, Peter and Cornelius, were thus national enemies. Contact between them was dangerous. Jews believed that they alone were the chosen people of God, and that these barbarian Romans were defiling God's holy land and ought to be evicted. There were plenty of people engaged in resistance (or terrorism) against them. The Jews also believed that to have contact with these Romans made them ritually impure. Although a good man himself, Cornelius was still an occupying soldier in a brutal conquering army. People who make friends with occupiers are despised as collaborators. At this time, tensions were rising, and the two nations were heading for conflict, a bloody war that would lead to the destruction of Jerusalem in A.D. 70. There should be no contact between these people.

And yet, by God's miraculous power, there is not only contact, but a most remarkable incident of reconciliation. Speaking by way of visions to both men, God instructs Cornelius to send to Joppa for Peter, and commands Peter to go to Caesarea, to the home of Cornelius. Alan Kreider has said that this little verse 23 is one of the most important in the whole of the New Testament,[3] and it is the pivot of Luke's narrative in the book of Acts: "Then Peter invited the men into the house to be his guests." Peter risked being defiled, he broke the traditions of his people, and he risked drawing accusations of betrayal from his neighbors who were already angry with Christians. Yet this act leads to Cornelius becoming the first named non-Jewish member of the church, showing the world that because Christ died to give life to all, the Christian church is for everyone of every nation, uniting old enemies in a kingdom of peace and demonstrating God's exciting plan for history. This is part of what Jesus meant when he said, "Blessed are the peacemakers." In a world with so much war, with so many barriers and divisions between people, this is why the Christian message is such good news.

THE CHURCH AND NATIONALISM

Unfortunately, although the church is uniquely placed to see beyond and act to overcome national divisions, through history it has often actually made nationalist tension worse. When conflicts over places emerge between different peoples, Christian churches have often concluded that God is on their side, and that God wants their nation or group of people to have that place. In recent times we have seen that to tragic effect, with Protestants and Catholics being the major split in the violence of Northern Ireland, and the Serbian Orthodox Church supporting and encouraging Serb warlords battling to control land in the wars that ravaged the former Yugoslavia. These are examples of what journalist Clifford Longley calls "chosen people syndrome," when a particular nation believes that God has specially chosen it to fulfill his mission through war.[4]

The tragedy and irony of this mixing of Christianity with nationalism was shown most clearly in World War II, when all sides believed that God was fighting with them and sought his assistance. British and American Christians prayed that God would grant them victory, that their countries and cities would not be overtaken by the Germans, so that Christian civilization would survive. The Russian Orthodox Church supported the atheist leader Stalin in what it saw as a struggle for the survival of Christianity against godless Germany. In Germany, evangelical Christians provided some of the staunchest support for the Nazis, as they believed that they were defending Christianity from the atheism of the Russians and the French and the backsliding of the English. The Finnish church loyally backed its state as it fought alongside Germany, and its leader even declared that the Anglican leadership had departed from the true faith by sending a message of support to the anti-Christ of the Soviet Union. Japanese Christian kamikaze pilots ploughed into American warships, and Catholic pilots of U.S.

bombers, ministered to by Catholic padres, dropped an atomic bomb on Nagasaki, a target whose epicenter was a Catholic cathedral at the heart of the largest Christian community in Japan. By 1945, the reputation of the Christian church as a single nation lay smoldering in the rubble of European and Asian cities.

However, when the church remembers the lessons from Acts 10, it is able to act as "salt and light" in a world full of dark nationalism. For example, in the 1960s Polish and German bishops began meeting with each other in a process of reconciliation.[5] These two countries still had bitter memories and unresolved issues from World War II, and were then in a nuclear stand-off in the Cold War tensions between the United States and the U.S.S.R. and their allies. Many influential groups in their home countries roundly criticized the Christians for being unpatriotic, for disregarding injustices of the past and for seeking forgiveness. That is very difficult to do when a country regards itself as the victim and the other side as a despicable enemy. Nonetheless, their fellowship began a process of dialogue and understanding that was to help smooth the way for political negotiations that led to final peace treaties in 1990 and 1991.

The evangelist Ravi Zacharias recounts that one of the most moving moments in his life was attending a fellowship meeting for Middle Eastern Christians in London. The organizers got an Iraqi and an Iranian Christian to pray for each other, at a time when their countries were at war; they then asked a Jewish and a Palestinian Christian to do the same, and so on. Ravi Zacharias described it as a foretaste of heaven, when people from all nations—even nations at war—unite together in faith in Christ.

RECONCILING NATIONALISTS?

I have been involved for some years with a project called the "Reconciliation Walk." It came out of a realization by evangelicals working in the Middle East that the reputation of Christianity and the work of the gospel were hampered by the spiritual legacy of the crusades. Those wars were also about special places. Muslim attacks against pilgrims going to towns such as Jerusalem and Bethlehem in medieval Europe had prompted the pope to call on Christian Europe to take up arms against the Muslims and retake these "holy places." Memories of the resultant bloody wars have played an important role in modern popular Muslim resentment toward Christians, a spiritual barrier to the work of the church and to good Christian-Muslim relations.

Sensing this, the Reconciliation Walk was started in 1996 by evangelical believers to bring Christians from around the world together to retrace the routes of the crusaders with a message of reconciliation. The message declared regret over acts done in the name of Christ, and sought forgiveness for allowing Jesus' name to be associated with hatred, fear and violence. Groups of ordinary Christians from around the world met Muslim clergy in mosques, and ordinary Muslims in their homes in Turkey, Syria, Lebanon, Palestine/Israel and elsewhere.

Like others on the walk, I spoke with both ordinary Muslims and senior religious leaders, and was amazed at how surprised, delighted and moved people were to meet us and learn about our message. They were also impressed that we were such a multiethnic group—even our small group had Christians from several continents. Many people said that we had radically changed their ideas about who Christians are—a message that found its way into the public sphere through media attention. In the same way, many Christians on the walk had their views of Middle Easterners and the political problems changed. Two examples of later stages of the Walk show the power of this vision of what the church is.

A pair of American Reconciliation Walkers in Lebanon met a

former mayor of west Beirut and got to know him during their time there. He told them that he was from a family of fighters, and that he knew from his family tree that eight or nine of his ancestors had died in the crusades. He himself had fought in the Lebanese civil war, against Christians, and he associated the cross with war. Driving the Reconciliation Walkers through a square in Beirut one day reminded him that he had fought American soldiers here, and was now passing through the same place with Americans as friends! He said that at first he had opposed the idea and values behind the Reconciliation Walk, and even the very idea that a good God could exist, but through meeting them he had come to conclude that it was a good idea. Indeed, he became increasingly touched by learning about God's forgiveness, eventually coming to England with a delegation to learn about and speak on the lessons of forgiveness after war.

In 2006, Reconciliation Walkers were invited to meet Sheikh Baraket in Gaza. He had been one of the founders of Islamic Jihad, a movement that used suicide bombing and other terrorist actions to oppose the Israeli presence in Palestine. He subsequently became critical of that approach and turned to more peaceful means of political engagement. When he met a group of Reconciliation Walkers in 2006, he told them how pleased he had been to hear about the project, that he had followed its progress and that he was delighted to have finally met its representatives. Indeed, he even quoted Jesus about forgiving one's enemies. He said that apology was the first part of the sentence, and now we must all—Palestinians, Americans, Britons, Jews—write the second part together, which is to speak up against evil and injustice. Who can tell what the spiritual and practical impact of all these lives touched by these simple acts by ordinary Christians will be? After all, who could have guessed the importance of Peter's traveling between those two cities all those years ago?

PRAYING FOR THE KINGDOM OF GOD

Projects such as the Reconciliation Walk are all well and good, we might say, but what can we, with busy lives, little money and no contacts, actually do? We may not even be able to spare ten days to join an organized trip to Israel/Palestine. Well, this passage from Acts 10 also shows that all true kingdom building starts with prayer, and that is something that everyone can do. Cornelius was praying, and in response God sent him an angel and opened the way to his salvation. This was an unlikely person praying in an unlikely place, but God heard him because his heart was right, and God will hear us too if we earnestly seek him. Peter was also praying when the vision appeared to him—a vision that went on to change the course of history. God turned Peter's idea upside down about whom God loved and who could be in the church, just as a real encounter with God will change our lives. He did not understand his vision at first, and stayed up on the roof thinking about it (verse 19). In the same way, prayer may often seem mysterious and confusing to us, but God always hears us and is using it to work out his purposes. By prayer, we become partners in God's peace-building work in the world.

One of the most amazing pray-ers I have met is an old lady named Florence. She is a tiny lady in her eighties who looks so frail but has bright, shining eyes, alive with the love of God. She has spent her retirement traveling the world praying for God's kingdom of peace—but she also prays at home, as can anyone. She was involved with praying for the Reconciliation Walk. I believe that God answered those prayers as we met many people and touched many hearts in the Middle East. We are all called to pray constantly, but prayer is often a way that retired, unemployed or less-mobile people can especially play a crucial role in building God's kingdom of peace.

If we follow Jesus Christ, we are part of God's great plan for history, which is to overcome the conflicts and barriers we put up between us and to draw all nations together in a worshiping kingdom of peace.

Learning to Be Peacemakers— in the Church and in the World

Please read Philippians 4:2-9.

Any Christian considering Jesus' declaration "Blessed are the peacemakers" during the War on Terror, or any other war, is likely to experience two very different emotions. The first is a conviction that these words have not lost any of their relevance since the day that Jesus first uttered them, that they are what the world needs to hear. The second is confusion or even despair about just *how* we put them into practice. Jesus did not declare the peace*lovers* blessed, because most people claim to be that, but rather the peace*makers*. To know peace with God in our hearts does not necessarily mean we are any good at being peace*makers*. How are we to learn the skills to be peacemakers in our homes, schools, workplaces, let alone in the sphere of international relations? As ever, Scripture comes to our aid. By considering Paul's letter to the warring Philippian church, we can begin to grasp the essential tools of peacemaking.

To be sure, our world is in need of peacemakers. From children arguing with their best friends, to long-running family or office disputes, right up to sports stars acrimoniously splitting from their teams, or politicians in the same party feuding with each other, "broken peace" is a story as old as the human race. Of course, this can happen in spite of the best of intentions: the Beatles famously sang, "all you need is love," but this did not prevent them from splitting up.

The War on Terror, too, is partially a story of broken relationships, although both sides would prefer to forget that. In the 1980s the United States supported al-Qaeda jihadists to fight the Soviet Union in Afghanistan, and British special forces helped with training. At the same time, Britain and America helped Saddam Hussein gain access to weapons of mass destruction for his war against Iran. Both friendships soured with the Iraqi invasion of Kuwait in 1990 and the subsequent U.S.-led war to reverse it in 1991. The fallout from broken relationships is felt from the school playground to the War on Terror.

CONFLICT IN THE CHURCH

Conflict thus appears endemic to our world. However, if there is one place where one would expect this type of conflict not to occur, then surely it is in the church, the peacemaking disciples of the Prince of Peace, who love their enemies and turn the other cheek. Sadly, the church has often been not a diffuser but an inciter of conflict. Down the centuries, Christians have proved unfortunately adept at falling out with each other and founding new churches. Aldous Huxley recounts the story from pre–civil war Lebanon of the Maronite Christian bishop who came into the ministry of agriculture to report on the state of the Maronite goat herds and said, "You will be glad to hear, your excellency, that we are doing very well with our goats in the mountains, but I regret to say the Orthodox goats are still causing an immense havoc!"[1]

However, conflict in the church is far from amusing, as anyone caught up in it will know. I was a member of a church that split into two, essentially along personal lines. With arguments erupting in services and accusations whispered behind backs, it was ugly and painful. A friend of mine grew up in a church and was put off by the infighting, citing as an example the modern "worship group" trying to impose new forms of singing with the traditional choir resisting. He said it got so nasty and personal that it helped to turn him against Christianity to this day.

I was once asked to preach from this text in Philippians on Mothering Sunday. As it is about a pair of fractious, quarreling women, Euodia and Syntyche, whose squabbling risked splitting the church, the choice of text seemed a bit ironic! However, this reminds us that the Bible is a handbook for real life. It does not deny that conflicts and personal frictions occur within the church. They are not unusual—in fact, if they are not there, it may mean that we are not really being church at all. Conflict is normal; it is how we *deal* with it that matters. And it is that very issue that Paul tackles head-on in writing this letter. We will consider two questions that his letter raises implicitly: "why does it matter if there is conflict?" and "how do we deal with conflict when it occurs?" Or, to put it another way, in the language of this passage, "why is unity important—why should we 'agree in the Lord'?" On this basis, we can begin to learn the skills of the peacemaker in the world.

WHY IS UNITY IMPORTANT?

"Agree with each other in the Lord" exhorts Paul in Philippians 4:2. Unity does not mean having the same opinion about everything. In his letters, Paul insists that his core gospel message is nonnegotiable, and that error must be corrected and heresies refuted. But what he calls "disputable matters" in Romans 14—such as scruples over holy days, fasting, food, drink and the like—are to be left to individual conscience, as long at they do not cause other believers to fall.

Unity is the central theme of the letter to the Philippians—unity
in the face of suffering and opposition. Although suffering can
sometimes bring groups together, it more commonly reveals tensions and creates divisions, as seems to have been happening in
Philippi. Paul therefore cites his own experience of hardship and
the example of Christ's suffering, and he urges the Philippians to
copy both models, and not to give up or split up. As Paul essentially
implores the Philippians, "if Christianity means anything to you at
all, make me happy by doing it in a unified way" (2:1-2).

Now, I must admit that I tend to be suspicious of anyone who
calls for "unity." The leaders of divided parties facing internal revolt, failing basketball coaches about to be sacked and heads of
state facing an election after an unpopular war urge the party, team
or nation to "unite behind them" for the common good.

But the church is not just another human organization. It might
have offices, administrators, bills to pay and annual meetings, but
it is very different. This is because it is brought into being by God.
What is the church for? In Ephesians 3, Paul says that God had a
secret plan for history that was revealed in Christ. This plan was
that people from every nation, old enemies like Jews and Gentiles,
would be reconciled to God and each other, united as "one body"
in Christ (Ephesians 3:6). Paul says that because of Christ's death,
our sin is forgiven and we have peace with God. He calls this message the "gospel of peace" (Ephesians 6:15), says that Christ "is
our peace" (Ephesians 2:14), that he "preached peace to [those]
who were far away and peace to those who were near" (Ephesians
2:17), and has brought us to "peace with God." The visible manifestation of this, the proof that God has done this, is the church.
Consider how Paul concludes his argument in Ephesians 3:10: "His
intent was that now, through the church, the manifold wisdom of
God should be made known to the rulers and authorities in the

heavenly realms, according to his eternal purpose which he accomplished in Christ Jesus." What a lofty and remarkable thought!

Next time you are in a church meeting, take a moment to look at the people sitting around you. Some of them will interest and excite you, others bore and annoy you. That is at the human level. But we must see deeper than that. The Bible says that our fellow Christians are like living stones, being built into a spiritual house where the holy Lord God Almighty dwells. Whenever we meet, we are part of God's great plan through all of history, the reason that the world exists. Seven centuries before Christ the prophet Isaiah foresaw the church, people like us, declaring that it would be called "a crown of splendor in the LORD's hand, / a royal diadem in the hand of your God" (Isaiah 62:3).

So it should be clear why unity matters. It is a visible vindication of God's work of salvation. As R. B. Kuiper wrote in his classic study of the church, *The Glorious Body of Christ*,[2] we do not create unity through committees and conferences—indeed, the unity that we create on an institutional level, if we do not really know Christ and adhere to true doctrine, is misleading. No, unity is a fact, a spiritual reality, and it is all God's work. Paul says that the church has one head, one spirit, one baptism, one faith, one foundation, and that it is one body. Nothing can destroy that unity, but divisions into countless denominations and visible splits obscure it. We do not create that unity, but we are called upon to demonstrate it. That is why Jesus prays in his great high-priestly prayer in John 17:21 for the unity of the church. Why? "That the world may believe that you have sent me." Or, as Paul says in Philippians 1:27-28, I want you to "stand firm in the one Spirit, striving together with one accord for the faith of the gospel, without being frightened . . . by those who oppose you." Why? "This is a sign to them that they will be destroyed, but that you will be saved—and that by

God" (TNIV). By demonstrating unity in adversity, we witness to the world that those outside the body of Christ are facing a lost eternity on account of their sin, but that those inside it have been gloriously saved from that fate by God's work in Christ. That is why unity matters.

HOW DO WE ACHIEVE UNITY?

Unity within the church is, therefore, a testimony to God's work of salvation. That is what the Bible teaches. It is exciting, even breathtaking, to realize that that is what ordinary Christians are doing whenever they meet together in unity to worship the Savior. That may be so, but what happens when we run up against the reality of sin in other people or ourselves? Have we ever gotten so angry with a church that we have felt like washing our hands of it and leaving to find a "better one"? Have we ever been so disappointed with the hypocrisy of Christians, the way that they compete and quarrel with each other, that we have felt like giving up? Have we ever messed up so badly, had an argument with someone, or upset someone, that we have felt hopeless and inadequate as a result? At such moments, we do not feel like "a crown of splendor in the LORD's hand." Likewise, it can be impossible to think of the person who has hurt us as being "a royal diadem in the hand of God." How do we square the reality of being living stones in the body of Christ with the apparent feeling of banging our head against those stones?

Paul's exhortation to Euodia and Syntyche guides us in how to be peacemakers in conflict situations in our church, at the personal, small group, congregational and interdenominational level. Following the work of church scholar Alan Kreider, who has much experience in both church and international peacemaking, there are five principles to draw out from Philippians 4:2-9.

First of all, Paul does not avoid the issue. It is quite a step to declare so openly that there is a problem between two named individuals, but Paul knows the potential unresolved conflicts have to damage the church. The Bible is so realistic here. Recall Jesus' instructions on what to do "if your brother [or sister] sins against you" (Matthew 18:15-20). Jesus does not indicate that this is surprising—he assumes that there will be problems in the church. If people share their lives only on a superficial level, nodding hello and chatting over coffee at the end of a service, or shaking hands and muttering "peace" when the minister tells them to, then there is little opportunity to sin against each other. But that is not church, at least not as the Bible sees it. In the church, people clash with one another, people sin. But we are to confront them Jesus-style, as he taught us: not to gossip, but rather confront them one-to-one, and then with others, until they listen. Jesus sketched out a picture of a functioning church, helping its members to develop good listening skills.

Some time back I asked a friend how his Bible study group was running. He said that they had had a difficult time, bringing up issues of conflict and disagreement that had been under the surface. It was not easy dealing with them, he said, but relationships were deepened and improved as a result. Alan Kreider wrote something very surprising: most congregations need more conflict, not less. Perhaps this is partly what Christ was referring to when he declared enigmatically that he came to bring a sword, not peace (Matthew 10:34).

Second, Paul is more concerned with the relationship than the issue. We do not know what issue they were arguing over. Various suggestions have been made. Perhaps it was to do with the factionalism we see in Philippians 1:15-18. Peter Oakes, who has studied the archaeological and social history of Philippi, suggests that it was sparked by economics, having to do with the social structure of a minority Roman population in the church owning an inordinate amount of wealth while the majority were poor.[4] However, this is really just speculation: we simply do not know what the issue was. Paul must have known. Epaphroditus had just come to Paul from Philippi and would have updated him on the situation, prompting Paul's letter. Imagine the temptation he faced to give a ruling and opinion. But he resists it. He does not take sides: it is important to him not that there is a winner, but rather that the relationship be restored in the Lord, that agreement and reconciliation be achieved. He is more concerned with the relationship than the issue.

BUILDING UNITY IN THE CHURCH

Paul's third principle for peacemaking in the church is that the whole church should be involved. Addressing a friend in verse 3, he says, "I intreat thee also, true yokefellow, help those women" (KJV). Paul has chosen someone who understands these people and their issues to act as a mediator. We should ask ourselves whether we are helping people in the church to be reconciled or whether we are hindering them, for example, by gossiping. What are we doing to develop our skills as peacemakers?

Fourth, Paul affirms these two women. He does not say to his "true yokefellow," "Take these old battle-axes, knock their heads together and sort out their wretched quarrel, so that we can all get some peace and quiet!" No, he stresses that they have both "contended at my side in the cause of the gospel," affirming their ministry. His love for this church and these people, Christ's people, shines through. When we have dealt with conflict recently, have we shown this type of love? Have we avoided name-calling and stereotyping, and looked for the good?

Fifth and finally, Paul keeps his eye on the bigger picture. He reminds them that they are working for a higher cause, they are part of this great church, that their names are written "in the book of life." Philippi, like other cities controlled by Rome, would have possessed a civil register recording the names of all citizens, those with the rights, privileges and duties of being full members of the Empire. Paul is making a point. The church of Christ is where our hearts lie, so we must not allow allegiances to anything else—political loyalties, classes, nations—to come between our relationship with other Christians.

PEACEMAKING IN THE WORLD

These verses, and the book of Philippians in general, therefore teach us that unity is important, and that we need to strive to demonstrate it. Together with Jesus' teaching in Matthew 18, they give us a method and series of principles to pursue in building peace in the church. But these principles are not only of use in the church—indeed, they can be the basis for the church's activity as a peacemaker in the world.

In a study for the Oxford Research Group in 2001, Dylan Mathews surveyed fifty cases of effective peace action by nonstate organizations.[5] Examples were taken from all over the world and included work done on conflict prevention, containment, de-escalation and reconciliation. Some of the cases detailed how wars were averted; others how full-blown violence was ratcheted down and eventually stopped. All of them were nonviolent, that is to say, "humanitarian" or "peacekeeping"; military interventions were excluded.

Mathews's book is a catalog of inspiring examples about how ordinary people have effectively stopped wars and killing. In his own analysis, the author says one of the remarkable findings was that nearly half the interventions were carried out by people with some spiritual basis for their activities. He considers this surprising, as religion played no part in the selection process of examples.

For Christians, however, this should not be surprising. In fact, twenty-one of the fifty cases cited explicitly stated Christian involvement in peacemaking, and I suspect that the actual number may be higher. Christianity provides strong theological grounds for insisting that peace in its fullest sense is possible (the death and resurrection of Christ and the eventual reconciliation of all things in him), and has at its heart the mandate for all Christians to be peacemakers. But, as Paul's letter to the Philippians (and other New Testament passages such as Christ's teaching in Matthew) shows, churches should be places where the basic skills of peacemaking are learned—skills that can then be transferred to the outside world. A number of examples from Mathews's book illustrate this powerfully.

Three cases of successful work by the organization Moral Re-Armament (MRA) are examined in Mathews's book. MRA was launched in the 1920s by an American pastor named Frank Buchman, in response to what he saw as the need for a "moral and spiritual awakening." In 1946 MRA organized a series of meetings between high-level French and German leaders, the first since World War II. MRA's approach stressed that peacemakers had to start the process of peacemaking and reconciliation with themselves, and that forgiveness was central. The effects were remarkable, as seen in the case of French Socialist member of Parliament Irene Laure. Her son had been brutalized by the Gestapo, and as a member of the Resistance she said, "I have so hated Germany that I want to see her erased from the map of Europe." However, her experiences at the conference led to a profound change, and she asked forgiveness of the German delegates for her attitude. This dumbfounded German delegates (including Konrad Adenauer, later the first chancellor of West Germany). Laure spent the next forty years traveling the world with her message of reconciliation and forgiveness. The

German government acknowledged the work of MRA as the foundation of postwar reconciliation and conflict prevention, and scholar Edward Luttwak later called it "one of the greatest achievements in the entire record of modern statecraft."

If the MRA's involvement in Franco-German relations was about reconciliation and possible future conflict prevention, Mathews cites the Lutheran World Federation's role in ending a long-running and deep-seated conflict in Guatemala. In 1952 the elected government of President Arbenz introduced land reforms to redress acute social and economic disparities between the two major ethnic groups. The U.S.-based United Fruit Company asked the CIA to intervene to prevent land redistribution. The CIA sponsored a mercenary army that overthrew Arbenz in 1954, leading to the formation of guerrilla movements seeking to achieve by force what Guatemalans had been unable to gain by political means. The military governments responded with massive brutality, destroying whole areas thought to be harboring guerrillas, and wiping out the populations.

In 1981 Reverend Paul Wee of America's Lutheran Church visited the country. Shocked at what he witnessed, he helped to assemble a small team in an attempt to bring the two sides together. After a long, slow process, leaders from both sides were brought to Norway for five days in an isolated chalet in picturesque surroundings. On the final evening a breakthrough came, when some of the adversaries discovered that they had grown up in the same neighborhoods. Tears and talk of shared visions followed, in a process that Wee described as the "dynamics of grace"—acceptance, prayer, confession, forgiveness, reconciliation. They stayed up all night, and a peace document was signed at 9 a.m. the next morning. There then followed years of meetings and dialogues between different sectors of Guatemalan society, orchestrated by church bodies. Eventually in 1996 a peace agreement was signed between the government and the guerrillas, ending thirty-six years of war. Other factors played a role (for example, the end of the Cold War stand-off between the United States and the U.S.S.R.), but the Lutheran World Federation's role was pivotal.

These examples, like countless more that could be raised, illustrate some of the essential principles of Paul's guidance to the Philippians—confronting not ignoring issues, respect for all sides, reconciliation and the role of outsiders in mediation. The church can play a unique role in peacemaking.

As we saw in chapter three, Paul calls his message the "gospel of peace," and Jesus proclaimed, "Blessed are the peacemakers." Few would disagree that our world of wars and terrorist bombers is desperately in need of peacemakers—but how do we rise to the challenge? It is in our local church congregations that we begin to learn the practices and skills of being peacemakers, living real lives of love with each other. We will then be better equipped to start to work out these lessons as "salt and light" in our families and workplaces and in the international family of nations.

The Battle of Jericho and the London Bombs

Please read Joshua 5:13—6:27.

We have been considering what it means to live as citizens of heaven. God's people have lived as citizens of heaven in two very different ways—as Old Testament Israel and as the New Testament church. In this and the next chapter we will look at what this difference means in practice, and how it affects the way we read the Old Testament during the War on Terror.

The account of the capture of the city of Jericho is one of the best-known episodes in the book of Joshua. As a story of faith in God allowing people to overcome impossible odds, of costly and risky trust in a God who miraculously intervenes to save his people, it is a splendid and inspiring example. It has always been a favorite story of preachers and Sunday school leaders trying to teach old and young Christians about faith.

However, reading it in the twenty-first century can be a disturbing and problematic experience. I found this when a scheduled sermon on this passage occurred just after the London transport bombings of July 2005. The account portrays Joshua as ordering genocide: with the lone exception of Rahab's family, every man, woman, child and animal must be slaughtered without mercy.

Reading this passage and reflecting on the murderous bomb attacks on London transport, or accounts from American military tribunals of U.S. soldiers going on the rampage and murdering whole Iraqi families in revenge for the loss of their comrades, we cannot avoid two very uncomfortable questions.

The first question is, does this set an example that we are to copy? Our immediate reaction may be to dismiss that as outlandish, but throughout history many Christians have indeed believed that it does. European crusaders rampaging through the Middle East and British invaders of North America wiping out Native American Indians drew heavily on texts from Joshua. "The sword of the Lord and of Joshua!" yelled Cromwell's troops as they rushed into battle against fellow believers in the English Civil War. In November 2004, U.S. military chaplain Kenny Lee held a service in a makeshift chapel in Iraq to mourn the deaths of eight marines killed in combat that week, and to bolster the survivors for an upcoming attack on the beleaguered city of Falluja. "Have I not commanded you?" he read from the book of Joshua, the biblical archetype of a military conqueror, "Be strong and courageous. Do not be terrified; do not be discouraged, for the LORD your God will be with you wherever you go" (Joshua 1:9). Christians have repeatedly used accounts such as this invasion of Jericho to assure themselves that they are wreaking terror on the world in God's name and with his blessing.

And then London, my birthplace, scene of the terrible suicide bombings of July 7. Muslims also hold Joshua as a prophet. Does Joshua's example justify those who would slaughter the innocent in London, New York and Madrid too?

It is exactly this question that causes so many people to reject religion. In 2005 Cambridge University hosted a packed debate on the existence of God. One of the main arguments used by the atheist speaker was the contention that the idea of a violent God reproduces violence in the world. He actually quoted this very text from Joshua as a prime example of how insidious religion is. We encounter this regularly in conversation with friends and colleagues too: religion is bad because it produces violence. Can this passage possibly be rescued from that charge?

JESUS AND JOSHUA

As well as the general issue of religion and violence, there is also a second question raised by this passage: how on earth does it relate to Jesus? As we saw in chapter three, in the Sermon on the Mount Jesus instructed, "Love your enemies and pray for those who persecute you" and "If someone strikes you on the right cheek, turn to him the other also." "Joshua" is the Old Testament equivalent of the name "Jesus," both meaning, "God is our salvation." But can we imagine two more different ways of dealing with enemies? In his book *Letters to a Young Contrarian*, journalist Christopher Hitchens uses this difference to dismiss Christianity.[1] He says that while the God of the Old Testament, the God of Joshua, teaches a violent ideology of ultravindictiveness, in the New Testament Jesus imparts an absurd code of ultracompassion, both of which are useless for governing a just society. Some liberal theologians and critics of religion have argued that the Old Testament basically consists of human ideas about God used to justify greed and violence, rather than being a divine revelation. But there are also, I think, many evangelical Christians who struggle with what they see as these two different images of God, and find it difficult to read certain sections of the Old Testament.

So two problems arise from an honest reading of this text: doesn't Joshua's example make the world a more violent place, and aren't Joshua and Jesus contradictory? These are significant objections, and it is vital that we understand and address them. However, we must begin by reminding ourselves of starting principles. "All Scripture is God-breathed," wrote Paul (2 Timothy 3:16), who described what we call the Old Testament as "the very words of God" (Romans 3:2). My own experience has been that as the Holy Spirit has brought the Scriptures to life for me, I have encountered the living God through them in a way that has transformed and renewed me. Therefore, rather than dismissing the Old Testament as a document of its time that has been improved on by human progress in the New Testament, we must understand correctly the relationship between the two. To address these two important questions, we will first step back and look at the big picture of God's plans through history, and then consider two aspects of Joshua's attack on Jericho and ask what they mean for us today: what was the goal of his attack, and why did he carry it out as he did?

GOD'S PLAN THROUGH HISTORY

In order to understand the significance of the book of Joshua for Christians today, we need to grasp the direction of biblical history. What is the meaning of history? In Ephesians 1 the apostle Paul talks about God's plans for all eternity. In verse 4 he says, "He chose us in him before the creation of the world to be holy and blameless in his sight." Holy means "set apart"; it means living for God as God wants us to live, lives that reflect his character— marked by purity, love, righteousness, compassion, justice, truth and peace. It means lives lived daily in his presence, worshiping him, knowing him better than anyone else, loving him and our neighbor. God takes sheer delight in such a holy people.

Through history God is building this holy nation. However, he acts with people differently at different times, and the major division of the Bible is between the Old and New Testaments, before and after Jesus' coming to earth. In the book of Galatians Paul explains the relationship between the law—the regulations for living in the Old Testament—and the gospel. He says that the law, with all its instructions and commandments, was put in place to "supervise" us until Christ came, to "imprison" or "hem us in" (Galatians 3:23-25). He compares us to children who need clear guidelines when they are young, until they are old enough to act sensibly by themselves. The turning point in this scheme was the earthly ministry of Jesus. Paul's doctrine of justification by faith is that we are made holy not by trying hard to obey laws, but because Jesus died for us on the cross. After Jesus ascended to heaven, he sent the Holy Spirit to help us live holy lives. Although the law remains a useful moral reference point, we no longer need it as a set of external rules and regulations to keep us holy. This is because the Holy Spirit dwells within us and enables us to live lives holy and pleasing to him.

That, then, is how God works through history. Understanding that helps us to reach a fuller understanding of Joshua's attack on Jericho—why he launched it, and why he conducted it in the way that he did.

THE REASON FOR JOSHUA'S ATTACK: HOLINESS

Why did Joshua kill everyone in Jericho? It was not to take territory and plunder a city to use. He did not enslave the men as laborers and the women as concubines, an aspect of warfare common at the time and also seen elsewhere in the Old Testament. Furthermore, he destroyed the major wealth and animals, preventing economic gain from his conquest. He not only burned down the houses but also placed a curse on their rebuilding, so his nomadic army was unable even to use it as a staging post or refuge, or resettle in it in the future.

Joshua was working from a very different logic, a rationale explained in Deuteronomy 20, the laws of war given by God through Moses for when the Jews conquered their land. They state that when the Jews attack cities outside Canaan, they are to offer the inhabitants terms of peace which, if accepted, mean that no one can be harmed. If these terms are rejected, then the Israelites can fight and keep plundered money, livestock, property, and women and children for themselves (Deuteronomy 20:10-15). Verses 16-18, however, reveal an entirely different commandment for cities within the boundaries of the Promised Land, such as Jericho: "However, in the cities of the nations the LORD your God is giving you as an inheritance, do not leave alive anything that breathes. Completely destroy them." The word translated here as "completely destroy" is sometimes translated as "devote to the Lord." It occurs in Joshua 6:21, "They devoted the city to the LORD and destroyed with the sword every living thing in it." It refers to giving over something irrevocably to God by utterly destroying it. It is a religious word, not a military concept. What is the reason for it? Deuteronomy 20:18 gives the answer: "Otherwise, they will teach you to follow all the detestable things they do in worshiping their gods, and you will sin against the LORD your God." This is the language of holiness.

Therefore, this "devotion" is not about economics, or a military strategy to create security. Nor is it about racial purity—whole groups of people could join the Israelites if they accepted Jehovah as their God. Indeed, in our passage Rahab and her family do just that. Nor is it primarily about justice, the punishment of evildoers, as there is no evidence that the cities outside Canaan were less sinful than those inside it. No, it is about holiness, the removal of the potential for the Israelites to be corrupted by the local population that would not bow to Jehovah and accept his law. These people worshiped their gods by sacrificing their children and had unjust and unequal socioeconomic orders, and before this point there had already been cases where the people of the region had seduced the Israelites away from worshiping God. The destruction of this "devotion" was intended to prevent that from happening again.

THE METHOD OF JOSHUA'S ATTACK: FAITH

If the goal of Joshua's attack on Jericho was holiness, why did he undertake it in the way that he did?

Joshua did not build siege engines. He did not bombard the city. He did not try to starve out the population over many months. He did not try to make alliances with other cities to help him against Jericho. He did not try to smuggle his spies back into Rahab's house and open a secret entrance to the city. All of these may have been sensible military strategies. Instead, he obeyed God's commands and walked the ark of the covenant around the walls for seven consecutive days, whereupon they miraculously fell down and he conquered the city.

We do not need to be professional military strategists to be aware that something rather unusual is taking place here. It is seen time and again in the Old Testament where praising priests are sent out leading the men into battle against a much more powerful foe, and God grants them a miraculous victory. Often God made his people intentionally weak before battle. Later in the book of Joshua we see Joshua burning chariots and hamstringing horses after capturing them in battle, because these were the main military technologies of the day and their absence put one at a considerable disadvantage. For the same reason, the Israelites were forbidden to form military coalitions with other states, alliances that could easily tip the outcome of any conflict. An identical logic is at work in Judges 7. When Gideon is about to face the

Midianites in battle, God tells him that he has far too many soldiers, and Gideon whittles the number of his men down from
32,000 to 300.

All of these strategies are absurd militarily. Imagine if the U.S.
secretary of defense appeared before Congress to answer a question about the strength of the army on the eve of battle and said,
"We are making good preparations; I have cut troop numbers to
one hundredth of their former strength, destroyed all our main-
line battle tanks and attack aircraft, and broken all our military
alliances, and have prepared faith leaders to march ahead of our
troops: victory is assured!" The very thought is comical. In the
Old Testament, God consistently made his people intentionally
weak in the human sense, so that they would depend on him in
faith for deliverance in a world of danger. God's holy people were
to be protected by him alone, as they obeyed him rather than following "common sense" military and political wisdom of the day.
That is why Joshua attacked Jericho in the way that he did.

FROM JOSHUA TO JESUS: THE CHURCH

We have seen that the outcome of Joshua's wars was holiness, and
the methods were designed to produce faith in a God who miraculously delivers. That helps us understand their relationship to the
New Testament teaching of Jesus and the apostles.

As the time of Christ drew nearer, we can see in the Old Testament a clearer idea of who the coming Messiah would be, and what
God's people would look like. Some prophets hinted that the Messiah would be rather different from Joshua. He would be a "Prince
of Peace" (Isaiah 9:6); his followers would not wipe out enemy nations but would welcome them as brothers and sisters, as people
from the entire world turned to God and beat their swords and
spears into plowshares and pruning hooks (Micah 4:1-3). As we

saw in chapter three, Jesus' life and teaching were the perfect fulfillment of this prophecy.

For a brief period in history, when God's holy people were represented by Israel in Canaan, they were confined and protected by
the law in one small space. When the time was right, God sent his
Son, Jesus, born of a woman whose family tree had been protected
by being part of that people, and, by the power of the Holy Spirit,
the church exploded out across the world, no longer "supervised"
by the law and tied to one territory. His people are still to be holy,
but we do not protect that holiness by wiping out nonbelievers or
removing ourselves from them and living in communes and drawing tight boundary walls around ourselves. On the contrary, in the
New Testament we are taught to live by the power of the Spirit as
"in the world, but not of the world." God gives us the power to resist temptation and live lives that not only please him, but display
him to those around us.

RADICAL HOLINESS IN ACTION

The Holy Spirit thus empowers Christians to live holy lives in a
way that Old Testament believers could not. When God's people
continue to live out that radical, risky holiness, God can use them
to have a significant impact on the world.

An example is that of John G. Paton, the great nineteenth-
century evangelical missionary to the New Hebrides islands in the
Pacific Ocean.[2] He worked among people whose culture was violent. They had been badly abused by other whites and were thus,
understandably, extremely hostile to him. Many of the friends he
made among them were killed. But he refused to leave or to use violence to protect himself against the people who tried to destroy
the work of the church. Many times people tried to kill him. But,
as his biographer put it, he never thought "of revenge or of shoot-

ing in self-defense. He trusted only in the Lord who had placed him there and to whom had been given all power in heaven and in earth." His patient work and example of a holy life led, after many years, to people being converted and accepting Christ. These new converts traveled to other islands preaching the gospel.

Litsi Sore was one of those who became a believer through the work of Paton. Queen of the Aniwans, she had an important social role as chief citizen. Tragically, her husband was killed by the chief of the neighboring Tannese people. Rather than organize a retaliatory expedition, she devoted her life to going to the Tannese, living among them and spreading the gospel. These are exactly the key themes of Joshua 6 correctly applied in the New Testament context: ordinary people empowered by the Spirit to lead holy lives that are attractive to others, and relying not on human means but on faith in a God who intervenes to save his people for their protection.

Another instructive example is that of Tom Skinner, a 1970s African American preacher.[3] As an angry young man and disturbed teenager resentful at the injustices that his community suffered, he turned to violence as a way to ground his identity. This is a story that is painfully familiar to us—for example, with the young suicide bombers who struck London. When still a teenager, he became the ruthless leader of a notorious New York gang and claimed to have knifed twenty-two people without a trace of remorse. He was a top high school student and brilliant strategist, studying classical texts on military theory to plot his own street warfare tactics. One night, he was listening to the radio as he planned a strategy for what he claimed would be the largest street war that New York had ever seen. The broadcast was about Jesus. He had been to church but had never really heard the gospel preached before. Now he was stunned to learn, as he put it, that God had taken Tom Skinner and put him (his sinful nature) on that cross, and that Jesus had shed his blood to forgive Tom Skinner's sins, deliver him from death and give him new life. He prayed there and then, committing his life to Christ that very instant.

Nonetheless, there remained the not inconsiderable matter of the gang. The next day there was a meeting of the gang, when he had planned to brief them on strategy for the upcoming battle. He told his dumbfounded audience about what had happened, that he had encountered Jesus and that he was leaving the gang. That was brave, as no one left that gang alive—he had personally made sure of that. Yet no one moved as he stood up and walked out past the seated gang members. A few days later he met a rival in the gang, who had said he had tried to get up and knife him but was rooted to the spot—and others had experienced the same inability to move. I believe that that was God's miraculous, intervening, saving power. Tom quickly developed a ministry of preaching and reaching out to gangs, and saw numerous killers saved in the fullest sense of the word, turning from death to life. He did not withdraw from his world, even though it was full of temptation and danger. Rather, his transformed and holy life, lived by the Spirit's power, amazed his former friends and enemies and proved infectious to them. He depended on God's miraculous power for deliverance from danger— the same power that God used to bring the walls of Jericho down.

Now, of course God does not always deliver his people from death, as we shall see in the next chapter. Christ himself implored his Father to spare him from the trials of the cross, but this prayer was not answered. The same is true for us, as we must often follow the path of our Master. All we can do is entrust ourselves to him and obey his commandments, and the rest is with him. We do well to imitate the prayer of John Paton when he faced imminent death, and "stand still in silent prayer, asking God to protect us or to prepare us for going home to His glory."

CONCLUSION: JOSHUA AND THE WAR ON TERROR

What are we to make of Joshua's attack on Jericho? His warfare was about holiness and faith, and was not motivated by politics, material gain or the claims of justice that drive modern warfare. Joshua's warfare was part of the law, a system along with temple sacrifices and food prohibitions that was weak and imperfect in that it was only "supervising" God's people in preparation for the culmination of history, Christ's appearance. The New Testament church, of which we are part, still protects holiness as passionately as Joshua did, and has the same faith in a miraculous God who intervenes to save us when we risk ourselves on him. However, it does both in a more perfect way. Everyone aching for meaning and reason in life can find all they are looking for and more by faith in the God who created this holy people.

The book of Joshua should inspire Christian warriors, but these are completely different from the warriors of Joshua's day. In the 1920s and 1930s, the British missionary Dorothy Hoare exercised a remarkable ministry in Japan.[4] A natural evangelist and gifted linguist, she entered the city of Yao in 1932. As her biographer wrote, it was her "Jericho," a city similarly full of idol temples and brothels set on a great plain. She led a "little band" of five other women in an "attacking force," engaging in prayer and evangelism in the city, strong in the consciousness that the "captain of the host of the Lord" was with them. In spite of initially encountering fierce opposition, through activities such as running Sunday schools, giving out tracts and helping the victims of an earthquake which left her house miraculously unscathed, a church was quickly raised up in the city. Indeed, Dorothy was regularly invited to reformatories to teach the Bible and hymns, as her gospel message changed the lives of young offenders that the authorities despaired of. As her biographer said, alluding to Jericho, the walls of Yao fell. The Christian church is no less militant than the church under Joshua, but the militancy of the gospel is altogether different, and altogether more powerful.

Dorothy Hoare understood well what many today fail to see. It would be a gross misunderstanding of the Bible to argue that Joshua's attack on Jericho can be a model for us today. Christians or Muslims who use it to justify bombing Baghdad or London make a grave mistake. As the nineteenth-century biblical expositor Bishop Ryle said, to hanker after the law now that we have the gospel would be to "light a candle at noonday."[5] Likewise, there is no contradiction whatsoever between Joshua's warfare and the enemy love of Christ and the apostles, between the Old and New Testament accounts of God. Both had the same intention—to produce a passionately holy and faithful community of believers—but the gospel has fulfilled and superseded the law under which Joshua operated.

John Paton, Tom Skinner and Dorothy Hoare exemplified the type of holy living that is at the heart of biblical faith. As Britain and America face murderous terrorists, our countries need more people like them. As Palestine and Iraq face both military occupiers and terrorists, they also need more of such people. This world needs people who are passionate and uncompromising about holiness, people who see God's standards and are prepared to live them out in the midst of violence and sin, without becoming polluted themselves. It needs people who dare to take Christ at his word, who dare to love their enemies and who dare to entrust themselves wholly to his protection. Are we ready for that challenge?

After Beslan

"THE CORDS OF DEATH ENTANGLED ME"

Please read Psalm 116.

In schools throughout the former Soviet Union, September 1 is "knowledge day," when parents and children, in their best new clothes, celebrate the start of the school year. As someone who has taught there, I have always enjoyed these occasions. For Beslan's School Number 1 in southern Russia, however, September 1, 2004, was an unimaginable nightmare. Thirty-two Chechen terrorists, continuing a long campaign to free their homeland from Russian military rule, took 1,200 schoolchildren, parents and teachers hostage. The siege lasted three days, when fighting between the hostage-takers, fathers of the hostages and Russian security forces led to the destruction of most of the school. When the smoke settled, 344 civilians, 186 of them children, lay dead.

How can we read Psalm 116 after this outrage? It is an unequivocal statement of confidence in a God who hears prayer and miraculously intervenes in our lives, delivering us from death. In verse 3 the psalmist says that the cords of death entangled him—he faced death, or something that reminded him of it. The image of entangling cords portrays death not as a passive state, but as a terrifying active force, grasping him, pulling him down, immobilizing him.

But then we see in verse 8 that he has been delivered from this deathly experience, as God mercifully answered his call for rescue. This was divine deliverance, pure and simple, culminating in a jubilant declaration of praise and thanksgiving to God (verses 17-19).

The happy ending to this psalm inevitably raises an uncomfortable question. It does not seem to fit with reality. To be sure, there are times when this may chime with our experience or the experiences of others around us. But what about when we call to God and he *doesn't* intervene? Christians in Russia and around the world prayed fervently for the children, teachers and parents in that school in Beslan. My own church prayer meeting did just that. But there was no deliverance for the hundreds of people who perished that day. Likewise, as we saw in chapter one, Christians from Iraq prayed fervently that God would deliver them from the expected American attack in 2003. He did not, and many perished.

So what are we to do with psalms like this? The church often privatizes them, applying them to inner spiritual and emotional experience. This is absolutely valid as far as it goes. The psalms are often unspecific about the troubles they describe, and have quite properly been used by believers down through the ages to provide solace and strength in personal crises. But if we apply this psalm *only* to inner experience, if we cannot make it say anything about the big stories of death in the real world, then we risk implying that Scripture is not relevant to the most important questions of our age, such as the War on Terror. At the same time, we reverse the apparent plain meaning that God intervenes in concrete ways when we face mortal danger. So, how can we read this psalm during the War on Terror, when confronted with terrorists, hostage-takers, cruel regimes and weapons of mass destruction? How can we read it when the "cords of death" really do seem to be entangling our world?

READING PSALM 116—WITH OLD AND NEW TESTAMENT EYES

To begin to understand this psalm, it is important to clarify what the book of Psalms is actually for. Psalms like these were not used by ancient Israel or the Christian church down through the ages simply as vehicles of private emotion. The psalter has been the hymn book of God's people in communal worship. In verses 14, 18 and 19 the psalmist tells God's deeds "in the presence of all his people," including "Jerusalem," the heart of power and national life, and announces that what God has done for him he will also do for other "simplehearted" people like him (verse 6). This psalm was used as part of a cycle of psalms read at the Passover feast, which celebrated God's miraculous deliverance of his people from Egypt, a concrete intervention in real history. That is the reference in verse 13 to "[lifting] up the cup of salvation": a cup of thanksgiving passed around at the festival. The psalmist is connecting his experience to the experience of the nation, saying that his God is the God whose characteristic it is to intervene on behalf of his people in response to their prayers. These psalms were used to comfort the Israelites as they faced the very real threats of war to their state down through the centuries—dangers not alien to our own world.

So how are we to use this psalm? For Christians, it is not unreasonable to read this psalm in the light of the crucifixion. The New Testament sees the Old Testament as preparing for and looking forward to Christ. For example, the temple system of sacrifices anticipated Calvary, and God preserved the line of people from whom Jesus would be born. We celebrate Communion, instituted by Jesus on the Thursday when he was betrayed and handed over to be killed. This psalm is one that the church has often used on the Thursday of Holy Week, giving the Passover and the remembrance of deliverance from Egypt a new meaning. Paul, in 1 Corinthians

10:16, talks about the Communion cup as the cup of thanksgiving, giving thanks for God's great deliverance in Christ as the new focal point of our worship.

As we saw in the previous chapter, God's purpose in history is to call a holy people, a new nation, to himself, for his glory. God had a covenant promise with Israel: he chose them as a special people, to whom he would give Canaan, and whom he would defend and deliver. This special state, with its laws to "hem in" the people, lasted until the time of Christ. God has made no such promise to Britain, America or Iraq, or anywhere else, so it is not appropriate to quote the Old Testament back to God and demand that he act to save "our country" and defend the honor of his name, as the psalmists were able to do. No, in Christ's death and resurrection, God made a new covenant with a new people, the church. He has promised us not that we would live in a small bit of land that he would defend, but that we would spread to every corner of the globe declaring his salvation.

Nor has he promised us that he would fight and kill our enemies. On the contrary, Jesus said that we would endure the same trials that he did, yet assured us that he would be with us always. When Christ died on the cross for our sins and rose again for our justification, the world changed radically. The power of death, with all its grasping cords, lost its sting, and the grave lost its victory. That does not mean that the victory has yet been finally worked out in history—we still get ill, suffer and die. That victory will not be finally complete until Christ returns, and death itself will be forever destroyed. In the meantime, we celebrate the eternal life that God has given us by proclaiming it in the church, joyfully taking up the "cup of salvation" and thanking God, as a testimony to the world.

DELIVERY FROM DEATH

If a psalm like this one was intended to be read in a communal context, how can it be meaningfully applied to our world, to the big stories of death that we, as the church, are faced with interpreting for our own citizens? It is helpful to consider some examples from the lives of real Christians who have wrestled with these questions. They show authentically Christian responses to violence and the type of delivery from death that the psalmist speaks about, deliverances that were based on the risky exercise of faith in the crucified and risen Savior. We will look at three issues that are pressing to us today: facing terrorists and hostage-takers, brutal regimes, and weapons of mass destruction.

Delivery from terrorists. Sarah Carson, an American missionary in Haiti in the 1980s, offers a compelling example of how to face terrorists and hostage-takers.[1] A paramilitary death squad, angry at U.S. intervention in their country, was sent with orders to kill the Carson missionary family. Sarah was frightened, but she welcomed them into her home, which surprised the terrorists. She read aloud from the Bible verses containing Christ's teaching on loving enemies. "That's impossible!" burst out the leader of the group. She replied that humanly it was not possible, but that with God's help it was, and insisted that even if he killed her she would still love him. The man was so astounded and impressed that he let her go, therefore risking his own life by disobeying orders. But it did not end there: the terrorists came to their church service that Sunday! Sarah led the service, as the male leaders (including her own husband) had been abducted. She invited the terrorists to come to the front of the meetinghouse for a welcome. The paramilitaries could not believe it, but did so, with their guns. Eventually, an old man came up to the front, as was the tradition, embraced the group leader and said, "We don't like what you did to our village, but God loves you, and you are welcome here." Everyone—including the women whose eyes were red from crying for their husbands whom these men had kidnapped—did the same. The leader, quite overwhelmed, took the pulpit and said that he had never before believed in God, but now could not deny that God existed because Christians loved their enemies. He promised to pay personally for anything the village needed in the future, and to help return hostages.

This enemy love was certainly not cowardice; on the contrary, it demanded a brave risk of faith in God's supernatural strength. It would have been far easier to hate them, or even to try to fight them by arming themselves. However, by taking the route that they did, the gospel was glorified by their genuinely Christian obedience to Christ and reliance on his power to deliver his people from the cords of death.

Delivery from brutal regimes. Second, what could faith in God's power of deliverance mean when his people are faced with a brutal regime? The story of Ugandan pastor Kefa Sempangi yields a remarkable and instructive example.[2] He obtained a Ph.D. in art history in the U.K. and returned to lecture in an independent Uganda, excited at the prospects for his new state. But the dream soon turned sour. Idi Amin, a thug used by the British as a military deputy to help maintain their grasp on the colony, took power and executed a reign of genocidal terror. Opponents were sadistically murdered, Amin's killers delighting in inventing ever more brutal and cruel methods of torture and murder. The property and wealth of ethnic minorities was plundered. Against this background, Sempangi became the pastor of a large church and was faced with the question of how to respond to this oppression. Although they debated it, church members rejected the use of violence to defend themselves. Instead, the church preached the gospel and served the poor, becoming a shining light in the darkness around it.

Following a service on Easter Sunday 1973, Sempangi was exhausted from hours of praying and preaching. He was also emotionally drained by the memory of a terrible cold-blooded murder in broad daylight that he had witnessed earlier in the week. Going into his church office alone, he was confronted by five of Amin's assassins, who had been sent to kill him. "We are going to kill you. If you have anything to say, say it before you die," announced the leader of the gang, his mouth twisted with hatred.

What would we do in his place? Wish that we had a gun, or an armed militia or foreign troops to defend us? Wish that we had never been a preacher in the first place? Sempangi wrote that he felt so sickened inside at the thought of death and never seeing his family again that he thought that he was going to drop dead with fear. But listen to what happened next, recorded in his own words:

> From far away I heard a voice, and I was astonished to realize that it was my own. "I do not need to plead my own cause," I heard myself saying. "I am a dead man already. My life is dead and hidden in Christ. It is your lives that are in danger, you are dead in your sins. I will pray to God that after you have killed me, he will spare you from eternal destruction."

The leader was amazed. He lowered his gun, told the others to do the same and asked Sempangi to pray for them. He was so dumbfounded and stunned at this that the assassin had to repeat the request. Sempangi told them to close their eyes—but he kept his open, as he thought that it might be a trick. He prayed that God would rescue them from death. He testified that their faces changed—they were not the same men who left the vestry as those who entered it. As he left, the leader observed, "I saw widows and orphans in your congregation. I saw them singing and giving praise. Why are they happy when death is so near?" he asked. Sempangi replied, "Because they are loved by God, who has given them life."

The title of Sempangi's autobiography, *Reign of Terror, Reign of Love*, is a fitting way to describe the testimony of the church in the world, declaring Christ's reign of love in our lives, in the midst of a reign of terror by the principalities and powers of this dark age.

Delivery from weapons of mass destruction. Finally, what might it mean for Christians to trust in God's power of deliverance from death when faced with weapons of mass destruction? The Cold War stand-off between the United States and the Soviet Union and their respective satellite states was a dangerous time; on a number of occasions, a potential nuclear war of global annihilation almost occurred. How did Christians respond? Well, of course, there were many different responses.[3] In the U.S. a group of Christians influenced the early 1980s decision of President Reagan to escalate the Cold War, believing that a nuclear war was recorded in Daniel and Revelation and must happen before Christ returned.

However, that was not the only response to the Cold War. I recently visited St. Francis House in Oxford, a Christian house of hospitality based on the model of the American Christian Dorothy Day.[4] During compulsory nuclear tests in New York, when everyone had to go and take shelter in the underground subway station, she and her friends refused, handing out leaflets questioning the government's strategy, saying that a nuclear war was unwinnable and that America needed to find more peaceful ways to conduct itself in the international arena. She was arrested each time, and often imprisoned. I once spoke to an elderly scientist, a believer, who had been involved with meetings of Western and Communist bloc Christians at the same time. The governments of both sides viewed them suspiciously, and even some churches saw them as disloyal to their political masters.

Were actions like these just gimmicks? I do not think so. Soviet archives only recently opened to historians have shown that the decision by Mikhail Gorbachev to end the Cold War was influenced by thinkers close to the Politburo who had been part of networks of Christians and scientists who had questioned the Cold War and argued that coexistence was possible. They provided ways of thinking that had a momentous impact on practical politics, delivering the world from that particular danger of death. When she was in prison, Dorothy Day read the psalms each night and said that they gave her strength. I would not be surprised if she often returned to Psalm 116. Christians are sometimes entangled by the cords of death around them, buying into a worldly culture of fear and hatred that believes that enemies can only be countered by an equal or greater show of weapons of mass destruction. Psalm 116, however, insists that the tragedies and cultures of death around us are not beyond God's control and not too powerful for his love to overrule.

These stories are offered not necessarily as models of behavior, but as illustrations of how people who believed in the power of a God who does intervene to save his own from death had real impacts on the world. Christians believe in Christ, the living God who told them to love their enemies and demonstrated how to do it, and who really does intervene to save his own when they are entangled by the cords of death. This faith liberates us to live in the breathless expectation of his miraculous action, freeing us from the culture of fear around us. The exciting task facing us, as the contemporary church, is to apply this truth imaginatively to the violent challenges facing our world today.

AND WHEN GOD DOES NOT INTERVENE?

We have seen that Christians are called to faith in a God who intervenes to deliver his people from the entangling snares of death. Now, it may be objected, that is all well and good, but what are we to make of it when God *doesn't* answer prayers and physically save us from death? To consider that, look at verse 15 of Psalm 116: "Precious in the sight of the LORD / is the death of his saints." The psalmist knows that although he has been saved, he may still die in the future in God's service, that sometimes God's saints do not have the deliverance that he has experienced. Ultimately, of course, we all die. But the psalmist affirms that the death of God's people is precious to God. The sovereign Lord uses even such deaths to his own glory, to advance his gospel of peace in a sinful world.

This truth that God uses the deaths of his precious saints for his glory is, ultimately, a lesson that Psalm 116 can teach us about the Beslan massacre. As the horror unfolded, Irina Gigoueva and her two sons, Mark, aged nine, and eight-year-old Arthur, were singing hymns in the sweltering gym of Beslan's School Number 1. A terrorist gripping a machine gun stood guard menacingly behind her. Irina held Arthur tightly and prayed aloud for God's intervention to touch the man. Hours later, shrapnel hit Arthur's head and his body went limp in her arms. After that, Irina carried on praying. Like her, many of Beslan's evangelical Christians, grieving the loss of children, mothers and fathers, prayed, comforted neighbors and urged forgiveness instead of revenge even as they buried their dead. Tensions between Muslim and Christian communities have existed at least since a war in 1992, and many in Beslan were calling for retaliation. Evangelical leaders called for forgiveness and peace. "It's not just by chance this happened. I think God wants to do a miracle here through the Christian community," said Taymuraz Totiev, pastor of the Evangelical Christian Baptist Church in Beslan. A glib, insensitive response? No, Pastor Totiev and his brother and copastor, Sergei, lost six children at the school. At their children's memorial service, Sergei stood and addressed crowd members who began cursing and vowing to take revenge. "Yes, we have an irreplaceable loss, but we cannot take revenge. As Christians, the Bible teaches us that we must forgive. Vengeance is in God's hands." Beslan's evangelical churches rapidly mobilized to visit the wounded in hospitals and distribute aid to hostages' families. They also plan to deliver Bibles to homes and expand Sunday school outreach. They set up a trauma counseling center, which they hope to turn into a youth center to equip young people with peacemaking skills. No wonder that a Christian leader working in the area said, "People are looking to Christians because they have hope."[5]

"People are looking to Christians because they have hope." What a fantastic testimony to the gospel lived out in real lives. In our current climate of fear in the War on Terror, do people in Britain, America, Palestine and Iraq look at us, at Christians, at you and me, and see a similar hope? As Christians, we have a message and a way of life that an aching, broken, violent world, held down by the cords of death, is longing to hear. We no longer need live in bondage to death, and we do not take death and the existence of warfare and violence as facts that determine all our actions and set the horizons of what we may count as reasonable action. We do indeed believe in a God who is not distant, but who is powerful to intervene and deliver his people from death, a God in whose eyes our deaths are not meaningless, but precious. It is imperative that we do not merely confine this to the realm of private experience, but proclaim it, together with the psalmist, in the presence of all the people.

PART 4

CHRISTIAN HOPE AND THE WAR ON TERROR

10

Who Is Winning the War on Terror?

Please read Jeremiah 32—33.

How do we know when we are winning and when we are losing? With something like a soccer match, it is always absolutely clear. I am a keen follower of the lowly English team Scunthorpe United, and am thus accustomed to knowing when a team is losing. I remember watching an epic clash between Scunthorpe United and Cambridge United. Up until the thirty-fifth minute of the game neither side had scored, so they were tied. At that point Cambridge scored and from then on was winning. In the eighty-eighth minute Scunthorpe scored, so the two teams were tied again. Finally, in the ninetieth minute Scunthorpe scored again to take the lead and, when the final whistle blew, were declared the winners. At halftime Cambridge was winning, but when time expired Scunthorpe had won. It is as simple and unambiguous as that.

The previous section discussed being citizens both of heaven and of earthly countries, and concluded on a note of hope. This final section takes up that theme of hope. Christian hope is more than wishing against the odds; it is a patient confidence that, in the grand scheme of things, we are on the winning side.

Of course, the War on Terror is not as clear as a soccer match. President Bush has said victory could take many decades, but God will surely grant it; Osama bin Laden regularly assures his followers that God will grant him victory soon. In Afghanistan it seemed that the Taliban government had been swiftly toppled in the autumn of 2001 when the United States invaded. However, by 2006 a resurgent Taliban was gaining more popular support, taking back control of swathes of territory from the U.S. and its allies. Likewise, in May 2003 President Bush helped land a military plane on an aircraft carrier against a banner declaring "mission accomplished," following a swift defeat of the Iraqi army. Four years later, intense fighting continues in Iraq, with over 2,500 American soldiers dead. How do we judge who is winning, and how will we judge who has won? When there have been no attacks on America for six months? Or twelve? When U.S. forces have withdrawn from Afghanistan and Iraq? Or the whole Muslim world?

This passage from Jeremiah is one that contains no such ambiguity. Written as the Babylonian armies under King Nebuchadnezzar terrorized Jerusalem, it boldly promises the people of Israel a future deliverance and prosperity, that they will be winners all around. Yet this was not merely about a particular war a long time ago. The fulfillment of this prophecy would be completed ultimately in Christ, and it thus proclaims news that is of universal concern and hope for humankind. It is especially instructive to revisit it when we, like Jeremiah, also find ourselves in a time of war.

SEEKING SALVATION IN WARTIME—JEREMIAH

Jeremiah was a prophet sent from God—in fact, one of the greatest prophets who ever lived. Now we might think that sounds exciting, that he was a fortunate man to have had that calling. However, Jeremiah himself would not lightly agree with us, for two reasons.

First, he lived during a time of war, in the early seventh and late sixth centuries before Christ. When this prophecy was given, Jeru

salem was being besieged by the Babylonian armies. They had devastated the Holy Land, systematically destroying its cities, plunder-
ing its fields and carting its people off into exile. Jeremiah was
stuck inside besieged Jerusalem, the great city of the Jews' greatest
king, David, but it too was about to be overwhelmed. If you were
to ask anyone in the city "who is winning?" the answer would be,
"the Babylonians."

Second, Jeremiah also suffered because he was alone. For years he
had prophesied about God's coming judgment. As we saw in chapter
four, he had warned the king and nobles of Jerusalem that God was
angry with them, that because of their sin—violence, oppression of
the poor and idolatry—God would destroy their kingdom. He urged
them not to take up arms against the invaders. But rather than heed
his message, they tried to silence him as unpatriotic and even kill
him, as they killed at least one of his few allies, fellow prophet Uriah
of Kiriath Jearim (Jeremiah 26:20-23). In chapter 32, we witness the
terrible fulfillment of that prophecy. Yet the people were not penitent
for ignoring him. Far from it, we see at the start of the chapter that
by this stage Jeremiah had actually been imprisoned by the king, who
did not want him to undermine the morale of the troops by his
gloomy prophecies. No wonder that on more than one occasion he
complained to God that he did not want to be a prophet!

So, humanly speaking, as chapter 32 starts the Babylonians are
winning, the Jews are losing, and Jeremiah's immediate future
looks very bleak. And yet, in the midst of this crisis, Jeremiah re-
verses the equation in the most dramatic way. He declares that, in
the big historical picture, the end-time results are not going to be
the same as the half-time ones. At some point in the future, he says,
God's people will live in peace and security, safe from invasion or
any enemy. Therefore, he is not afraid, he is not pessimistic, he can
look at all that he sees around him and have hope.

How can he be so hopeful? He was not a natural optimist. We learn from his book that he was a highly emotional man who did not respond calmly to opposition and was given to bouts of serious depression, writing great lamentations to express his pain and misery to God. But he had a revelation from God, a unique one:

"The days are coming," declares the LORD, "when I will fulfill the gracious promise I made to the house of Israel and to the house of Judah.

"In those days and at that time
I will make a righteous Branch sprout from David's line;
he will do what is just and right in the land.
In those days Judah will be saved
and Jerusalem will live in safety.
This is the name by which it will be called:
The LORD Our Righteousness." (Jeremiah 33:14-16)

God had told him that eventually he would send his own agent, the "righteous Branch," to restore the kingdom and save his people. This man would be a descendant of King David, but he would also be God—Jeremiah calls him "The LORD Our Righteousness." The other prophets also looked forward to the coming of this Messiah. We know, with the benefit of hindsight, who this was—Jesus: Jesus, born in Bethlehem, of the royal line of King David, the one whom Israel had waited for; Jesus, the one who would die for his people and all the world, taking their sins as his own and paying for them with his blood, that we might become the righteousness of God in him—be made holy and fit for heaven; Jesus, who would offer true peace and security to his people, indeed, to the whole world.

JESUS' EVERLASTING EMPIRE

It is true, this restored kingdom that the prophet foresaw was not like the old one. In fact, it was not like any other. It did not have palaces, armies, cities and territory. It was proclaimed by a little baby born to poor parents in a barn. Jesus never enjoyed pomp and wealth, nor did he frequent the halls and palaces of the powerful. He didn't write a book and was not respected by the opinion formers of his day. In the end he was crucified like a defeated rebel. It looked as though he had lost, and the kingdoms of the world had won. Yet the kingdom that he established is the only one that will endure. It has already outlasted the Roman Empire and a host of other great military powers.

It will also outlast those powers struggling for supremacy in the War on Terror, with their grand moral visions of a future political order. In his National Security Strategy of September 2002, President Bush announced a policy to act preemptively to prevent any potential rival power from developing the military means to threaten American supremacy.[1] This was a statement of permanent military and political supremacy, and was widely interpreted by supporters and critics alike as being about "American empire." Likewise, in his "letter to the American people" written around the same time (see Study Guide 1), Osama bin Laden promised to defeat America militarily and bring about its destruction, when eventually the reign of his version of a just and peaceful Islamic state would be established on earth. However, the kingdom reign of Jeremiah's "righteous Branch" will outlast any pretension to universal empire by any human state or organization, no matter how powerful its armies or how lofty its ideals.

This kingdom is present wherever people believe in Christ and call out to him, trusting that his death has made them holy and that he will preserve them in eternal life beyond the grave. We will see the final evidence of it when Christ returns to judge the earth on the last day. Then, every supposed great person from every earthly kingdom will bow before him. Kings and queens, presidents and prime ministers, terrorists and soldiers, bishops and mullahs, football stars and journalists—every one of them will bow at the name of Jesus, and every one confess that he is Lord (Philippians 2:10-11). As in Jeremiah's day, the world around us looks like one where the biggest men with the biggest weapons and the most money make history, where they win. But that is an illusion: like Jeremiah, we know that the real story is the story that God is building, using ordinary people like you and me.

What, then, are we to make of a world of wars that seem to lack winners, when every side claims that the future belongs with them? The Christian gospel, from the days of Jeremiah and the prophets down to our time, has not changed, and gives a glorious answer. The kingdom of God, foreseen by the prophets and proclaimed by Christ and the apostles, is the only everlasting kingdom, the only eternal hope, for us and our world.

SEEKING SALVATION IN WARTIME—MALCOLM MUGGERIDGE

The gospel, glimpsed by Jeremiah but revealed in Christ, thus proclaims a different type of kingdom, the only eternally enduring kingdom. To enter into it by faith in Christ is to have one's worldview turned upside down. That was the experience of the late Malcolm Muggeridge. He was one of the greatest British journalists of the twentieth century, and understood the workings of tyranny better than most. He reported on many of the biggest stories of the twentieth century—the rise of fascist Italy and Germany, Stalin's tyranny, the collapse of British military imperial power, and American defeat in Vietnam. Later in life he became a Christian, entering into Jesus' kingdom. Yet it was not the powerful statesmen and armies that made the greatest impact on him, but one weak woman whom he interviewed—Mother Teresa of Calcutta—and her winsome service for Christ. Listen to what he said about history:

We look back upon history, and what do we see? Empires rising and falling. Revolutions and Counterrevolutions. Wealth accumulated and wealth dispersed. Shakespeare has written of the rise and fall of great ones, that ebb and flow with the moon.

I look back upon my own fellow countrymen, once upon a time dominating a quarter of the world, most of them convinced, in the words of what is still a popular song, that the God who made them mighty, shall make them mightier yet. I have heard a crazed, cracked Austrian announce to the world the establishment of a Reich that would last a thousand years. I have seen an Italian clown say he was going to stop and restart the calendar with his own ascension to power. I have heard a murderous Georgian brigand in the Kremlin, acclaimed by the intellectual elite of the world as wiser than Solomon, more humane than Marcus Aurelius, more enlightened than Ashoka. I have seen America, wealthier and in terms of military weaponry, more powerful than the rest of the world put together, so that had the American people so desired, they could have outdone a Caesar, or an Alexander in the range and scale of their conquests.

All in one lifetime, all gone with the wind. England part of a tiny island off the coast of Europe, threatened with dismemberment and even bankruptcy. Hitler and Mussolini dead, remembered only in infamy. Stalin a forbidden name in the regime he helped found and dominate for some three decades. America haunted by fears of running out of those precious fluids that keep their motorways roaring, and the smog set-

tling, with troubled memories of a disastrous campaign in
Vietnam, and the victories of the Don Quixotes of the media
as they charged the windmills of Watergate. All in one lifetime, all gone with the wind.

Behind the debris of these solemn supermen and self-styled
imperial diplomatists, there stands the gigantic figure of One,
because of whom, by whom, in whom and through whom
alone, mankind may still have peace: the person of Jesus
Christ.[2]

Jeremiah saw this person of Jesus Christ from a distance. Muggeridge, like all of those born in the time since Christ's earthly ministry, had the privilege of encountering him personally. He, and he
alone, remains the hope for a war-torn world, and his kingdom is
the only one that will endure long after the world has forgotten
who won the War on Terror, and even who Osama bin Laden and
George W. Bush were.

LIVING PROPHETICALLY THROUGH A WAR OF TERROR

We have seen that Jeremiah could find hope in the midst of the terror
of war because he saw Christ, whose kingdom would last forever.
But what did he actually *do?* What are we to do? As we saw in chapter four, Jeremiah did not fold his arms complacently and say, "I told
you so!" He mourned, and so should we. But he did more than
mourn: he acted to demonstrate his faith. How? By buying a field!

We learn from Jeremiah 32 that during this siege, while still in
prison, the prophet enacted a rather peculiar business transaction.
He bought a field at Anathoth from his cousin Hanamel. He paid
seventeen shekels of silver, sealed the deal and had it witnessed.
Why did he do this? The land was overrun by the enemy, and the
destruction of the nation was about to occur. What use would legal

documents be if the whole system is overthrown? Why buy land when someone else has taken it by force? The answer is that God ordered it, to reveal his plans for the future, when economic life would return to normal under God's blessing. This was an act of faith, a concrete, simple, human act that testified to the world of his faith in a God who securely held the future, whose grace would outlast the terror of war.

That is what we are called to do in our day, too. Although God has not fully established his kingdom on earth yet, and although Christ's everlasting rule of justice and peace may seem impossible to imagine in the War on Terror, it is real, and we point others toward it by simple, prophetic acts of faith, as Jeremiah did by buying his field.

BUYING FIELDS IN THE MIDDLE EAST

Jeremiah not only proclaimed the hope of the gospel but acted in faith to demonstrate its reality. What would that look like for us? Different Christians will reach different conclusions, but two examples will suffice as possibilities.

The first is the work of the Foundation for Reconciliation in the Middle East, headed by Anglican minister Canon Andrew White. It has sought to reduce religiously inspired hatred, intolerance and violence in the Middle East. It has brought religious leaders together to dialogue. For example, in 2002 it organized the signing of the Alexandria Declaration for Peace in the Holy Land, chaired by the archbishop of Canterbury, a grand imam and a chief rabbi. It has orchestrated ongoing contacts between warring sides, for example, keeping Muslims and Jews in Palestine/Israel and Sunnis and Shiahs in Iraq talking when other channels of communication have been suspended. It has been involved in negotiating the lifting of sieges and the release of hostages in Palestine and Iraq. Andrew

White has achieved this by patiently listening to all sides and acting to bring them together—at times when it seemed impossible. This has been backed up by a network of faithful pray-ers linked to Coventry Cathedral's International Centre for Reconciliation.

The second example is the work of Christian Peacemaker Teams (CPT).[3] They take a very different approach than the Foundation for Reconciliation. They describe themselves as "the Lamb's army," walking into battle zones "armed only with the Gospel of Jesus Christ, and him crucified." Their essential goal is "violence reduction." They seek to do this by "getting in the way," accompanying civilians in conflict zones, and literally standing between them and soldiers who might try to shoot or beat them. They also work with local religious groups and other organizations to promote dialogue, undertake human rights monitoring and report about what they have seen to the world media to raise awareness. The organization shot into the international media focus in 2005 when Norman Kember, an elderly British Christian and retired university professor, was kidnapped (and later released) while working for CPT in Iraq. The focus of the Iraq work had been documenting and publicizing detainee abuse, and fostering nonviolent practices of violence reduction. Norman Kember's work demonstrated to Iraqis that Christians in the West care about their plight, and do not all support the invasion and occupation that they associate with so much hardship.

The wisdom of CPT's dangerous work has been doubted by many, including Andrew White of the Foundation for Reconciliation in the Middle East. Likewise, Andrew White's approach to questions of conflict in the Middle East has been criticized for compromises involved in negotiating with certain politicians. While I would not necessarily endorse all aspects of either project, both, in their own ways, are equivalents of Jeremiah's purchase of a field.

They are small acts that may seem futile on the face of it, undertaken against backgrounds of despair and hopelessness. Yet they demonstrate to the world that, in spite of the dramas of war and terrorism that darken our age, the peace and justice of the kingdom of the "Lord Our Righteousness" alone will endure forever. They also demonstrate that the way we live and act is determined not by fear of war and terrorism, but by a Christian hope that we are truly on the winning side, and we will only play by its rules.

11

Christian Hope and Suicide Bombers

Please read Acts 28:17-31.

How do we cope with disappointment and tragedy in life? How do we manage when trouble and pain unexpectedly afflict us, when we are fearful for the future and do not know what will happen? How do we not only get on with daily life at such moments, but live it joyfully and hopefully?

These are important questions, because from time to time we all have to face them. We face them as individuals, and also as societies. The War on Terror has led to widespread fear. After the September 11 attacks, Osama bin Laden thanked God that America was "filled with fear from the north to south and east to west," which was an apt description, as those images of planes suddenly striking buildings became lodged in our minds. The U.S. military attacked Iraq in 2003, promising a strategy of "shock and awe," and psychiatrists have reported that this fear indeed led to disorders among children, and no doubt among adults too. I was once speaking on the telephone to friends in the Palestinian city of Ramallah who were frightened at the sound of explosions from Israeli attacks that I could hear in the background. Traveling on the London Underground a few days after the bombings of July 7, 2005, it was impossible not to feel nervous and indeed suspicious of people who might be potential suicide bombers. Fear for the future, and the suspicion, polarization, even hatred that it breeds, are all around. How do we as societies, and we as Christians in those societies, face such times of national crisis?

In order to be of real relevance, a belief system must not only be able to make abstract arguments and recommendations, but genuinely be able to assist ordinary people in such circumstances. The Bible contains many cases of Christians coping with life's trials, which are written down for our guidance and instruction. In the conclusion to the book of the Acts, we find one such example in the final record of the life of the apostle Paul.

PAUL'S PREDICAMENT

At this point in the narrative of Acts, Paul is in prison awaiting trial in Rome. His route to this predicament was a long and tortuous one. In Jerusalem he was attacked by a mob who were angry that he preached the Christian gospel. He was arrested by the Roman authorities, who found no fault in him. However, to protect him from a gang who had planned to murder him, he was sent for further trial at Caesarea, where he was imprisoned for two years. In order to avoid being sent back to Jerusalem, he appealed to Caesar and so was dispatched to Rome. In Rome he was placed under house arrest for another two years.

We can only imagine how frustrating this whole debacle of Roman justice must have been for him. Here was the apostle Paul, the great traveling preacher and evangelist. His was a life on the road, visiting new towns to plant churches, and revisiting those that he had established earlier to check on their progress. Yet, here he was in prison! Having been detained for four-and-a-half years, he must have longed to be traveling again and spent many hours thinking about all the places that he wanted to go to, and the people he wanted to see. Apart from frustration, there may also have been

confusion about why God had allowed all this to happen to him.
There is no evidence that Paul felt this, but certainly, from his letters, it appears that some of his friends were highly discouraged on
account of the time he spent in prison. He had appealed to Caesar
to end his imprisonment and no doubt was hoping for a quick trial.
Two years on from this appeal, however, he was still languishing
under house arrest. What a wretched situation!

. We may find ourselves in similar situations. Granted, we are unlikely to be arrested in Britain or America for preaching the gospel,
although Christians are commonly harassed or detained in majority Muslim countries and communist or secular dictatorships.
Nonetheless, we can still find ourselves trapped in various ways.
We may be trapped in jobs that we do not like, or in unemploy-
ment; or trapped in ill health, as our bodies fail us and prevent us
from doing all the things that we want to. We can be trapped in disappointment, as life does not turn out the way that we dreamed it
would; we may be trapped in relationships that seem to constrict
and confine us. As a society, we can also be trapped in fear. In the
aftermath of recent violence, who would blame a British person for
being afraid of being suddenly murdered in a terrorist attack, or an
Iraqi for fearing being tortured or killed by American soldiers or insurgents in Iraq?

PAUL'S RESPONSE

Humanly speaking, Paul was trapped in a situation that not only
apparently hampered his ministry, but also had the potential to lead
to his execution. What did he do? The last verse of Acts 28 records
that: "Boldly and without hindrance he preached the kingdom of
God and taught about the Lord Jesus Christ." He did not retreat
into himself and wait for better days. No, he was bold in preaching
the gospel and telling people about Jesus. This was his customary

response. Some years earlier, when behind bars in Philippi after being beaten for preaching the gospel, at midnight he and his companion Silas were singing. Paul was bold.

Why was Paul able to respond in such an apparently superhuman way? Some people, of course, see Christianity not as divine grace but as a matter of personality or even genes. They might therefore say that Paul's response was simply a manifestation of his particular character, that he was by nature either an optimist or a stoic. By the same argument, others of different temperaments cannot hope to share his faith, and so would be better suited to adopt some other stance on life. However, it is easy to demonstrate from Scripture that this is not true.

First, Paul was not an optimist, not one of those bright and cheery people who never get affected by woes or concerns, who are sure that everything can only get better and so there is no point worrying too much about it all. Optimism can be useful if you are playing football or approaching exams, for example, but it can also be groundless wishful thinking. Paul was no optimist. In his letter to the churches at Corinth, he tells them, "when we came into Macedonia, this body of ours had no rest, but we were harassed at every turn—conflicts on the outside, fears within" (2 Corinthians 7:5). Again, when visiting Corinth for the first time, he went "in weakness and fear, and with much trembling." We see from his letters that he was a man who was sensitive to criticism, who could be upset when people said negative things about him.

Well, if he was not an optimist, was he a stoic? Stoicism is the attitude that says, "What will be, will be, and I am not going to let it get me down, but will soldier on regardless." It is typically British. We saw it after the "7/7" bomb attacks on London's transport system in 2005. People defiantly said, "We aren't going to give in to terrorism, we are going to go about our lives as normal, and not give these people the satisfaction of frightening us." The newspapers called this the "spirit of the Blitz," recalling the resilience of World War II Londoners refusing to be cowed and going about their daily life as German bombs rained down. No doubt stoicism is useful in situations like that, but the Christian position is very different. Stoicism is negative; it's a grim determination to accept whatever happens and not allow it to spoil one's ease. Christianity, on the other hand, is positive. It joyfully embraces a vision and hope that allows a person to rejoice in affliction and, like Paul and Silas, to sing in prison (Acts 16:25).[1]

Paul's position, the Christian position, is that we believe something about the world that changes the way we act in it. What is that? We see it in the last verse of the book of Acts: "Boldly and without hindrance he preached the kingdom of God and taught about the Lord Jesus Christ." Paul believed that the Almighty God, the Creator and Sustainer of the Universe, was building his kingdom, was working in the world to save humankind, and was therefore at work in Paul's life. He believed that this was not some vague, general principle, but was made real by the Lord Jesus Christ, the Man who was the Son of God and who had encountered him on the road to Damascus and transformed his life. Therefore, life and all that befell him was not chance, but directed by a sovereign Lord who "in all things . . . works for the good of those who love him, who have been called according to his purpose" (Romans 8:28). It was no wonder that he could be bold in prison.

LESSONS FOR THE WAR ON TERROR

As we have seen, Paul's attitude to the calamities that befell him had nothing whatsoever to do with his personality, but everything to do with his belief in the Lord Jesus. This has been evidenced in believers down through the ages but is well illustrated in the life of a nineteenth-century American, Horatio Spafford.[2]

Spafford was a successful lawyer and family man, wealthy, and a friend and supporter of evangelist D. L. Moody. He was a devout church elder and a supporter of the slavery abolition movement. But disaster struck. The Chicago fire of 1871 wiped out his property holdings, and this was followed soon after by the death of his son. In 1873 his wife and daughters were to go to Europe to take a much needed break. However, in the mid-Atlantic their ship, the *S.S. Ville Du Havre*, collided with another one and sank. His wife, Anna Spafford, was rescued, but their four daughters drowned. Thus, Horatio Spafford went from being a very wealthy man with a big family to a poor childless one. So what did he do? He did not say, "I must be cheerful, it is not as bad as it seems." No, such optimism is insulting and foolish. Nor did he say, "I must not give up. I must call on my reserves of courage and be a man." No, that is stoicism, and, as Lloyd-Jones reminds us, this man was a Christian, not a stoic. No, he wrote the words of the great hymn:

When peace like a river attendeth my way,
When sorrows like sea billows roll;
Whatever my lot, thou hast taught me to say,
It is well, it is well, with my soul![3]

A similar attitude was displayed by Reverend Mehdi Dibaj, a Muslim convert to Christianity, who was brought before an Islamic court in Iran in 1993 and charged with abandoning Islam, a "crime" punishable by death. This is an extract from the defense that he made to the judges presiding over him:

The love of Jesus has filled all my being and I feel the warmth of His love in every part of my body. God, who is my glory and honour and protector, has put his seal of approval upon me through His unsparing blessings and miracles. . . . The good and kind God reproves and punishes all those whom He loves. He tests them in preparation for heaven. The God of Daniel, who protected his friends in the fiery furnace, has protected me for nine years in prison. And all the bad happenings have turned out for our good and gain, so much so that I am filled to overflowing with joy and thankfulness.[4]

He wrote from prison, "I am filled to overflowing with joy; I am not only satisfied to be in prison . . . but am ready to give my life for the sake of Jesus Christ." When faced with the terror of a brutal regime, he was neither optimistic nor stoical; his response was absolutely Christian, informed by what he knew of God from the Bible, made real in his own experience by the Holy Spirit.

The faith and joy of these men, and the solace that they found in Christ, is remarkable. But we have access to the same grace and know the same Savior as they did. If we are merely optimists, we will find ourselves overtaken by tragedies that befall us, for in reality we all die and sometimes things go irrecoverably wrong. If we are only stoics, we will grind through life increasingly deaf to the joy and wonder of existence, and the assurance that another world is possible. But Christians approach life altogether differently. They know that God really is at work in the world. They know that ill health, frustration, loneliness, war and terrorism are not the last words in history. They also know Jesus Christ is with them as their savior, redeemer, counselor, lover and companion. Such a person is never trapped, no matter how helpless they may feel. They know that God is working all things together for their good, and they know that they can be effective for that kingdom however difficult their circumstances. Furthermore, they know that afterward they will rise to glory.

CHRISTIAN HOPE AND SUICIDE BOMBS

Christian faith, therefore, enables ordinary women and men to be joyful and hopeful even when facing the darkest situations. Of course, this is not to downplay or ignore the threats of terrorist bombs and warfare. Yet even when the worst does occur, Christian faith in God's overruling power offers a hope that no mere optimism or stoicism can match. One concluding example illustrates this, involving someone I met in a certain Muslim country. Aisha converted to Christianity from Islam when she was a student, but her parents wanted to force her into an arranged marriage with a Muslim man. She and her fellowship had prayed fervently for deliverance from this fate, but her prayers were not granted, and the marriage went ahead. Aisha moved to another city, where her husband Abdul worked as a policeman, and she fell out of fellowship with other Christians.

That was some years ago. Abdul was recently badly wounded in an Islamic terrorist suicide bomb attack on the security services. He was only able to find peace and go to sleep when his wife prayed for him at his hospital bed. During this time she managed to reconnect to other local believers. They visited and prayed for Abdul, who subsequently committed his life to the Lord Jesus and, at last report, was praying and reading his Bible every day. God, it seems, "in all things works for the good of those who love him, who have been called according to his purpose," even in terrorist attacks.

12

Conclusion
THE CHURCH AND THE WAR ON TERROR

THE GOSPEL AND THE WAR ON TERROR

The attacks of September 11, 2001, and the subsequent War on Terror are commonly discussed as something *new*, as a turning point after which "the world will never be the same." Politicians and commentators frequently speak about new dangers, new awareness of vulnerabilities, new kinds of weapons and wars, new alliances, and new categories of prisoner. Undoubtedly on the political and military level, there may be some truth in such language. Of course, for people wounded or bereaved by any aspect of the War on Terror, much will have changed personally. However, for the Christian trying to make sense of the world, these developments present nothing fundamentally new. As American theologian Stanley Hauerwas said, the world changed most profoundly in A.D. 33 when Christ was crucified and resurrected, when death lost its sting and the grave lost its victory (1 Corinthians 15:55 KJV). The challenge is to interpret every other event in history, including 9/11, 7/7, and the wars on Afghanistan and Iraq, in the light of A.D. 33.

The Christian gospel teaches us that humanity's main problem is that it has rebelled against God, separating itself from its Maker. This is known as "sin" and, as Paul wrote, "the wages of sin is death" (Romans 6:23). This means that when we disobey God and attempt to live life without his law, we inevitably bring negative consequences upon ourselves and others. War is no exception. It is not the condition that God desires the human race to live in; it is a denial and reversal of his good plans for humanity. As Martyn Lloyd-Jones taught, it is a manifestation and a consequence of sin. It is a manifestation or symptom in that it demonstrates a refusal to obey commands such as "do not kill" and "love your enemies," a refusal to treat with proper respect those made in the image of their Creator. It is a consequence in that it is something terrible that we have brought upon ourselves by this very disobedience, something that we were not meant to experience and indeed need not have endured. Theologically, the War on Terror is no different from any other war. God sorrows over war and is angry that it exists, and our reactions should be the same. But we should not be surprised or caught off-guard by it.

However, as Paul continues, "the wages of sin is death, *but the gift of God is eternal life in Christ Jesus our Lord.*" The root cause of war is sin, and the Christian gospel deals with sin. By Christ's death and resurrection, every man, woman and child can be made right with God ("justified"), be forgiven and find peace with God and other people as broken relationships are restored. Victory over sin and death was achieved at Calvary. That victory will finally be worked out in history when Jesus Christ returns to judge the living and the dead, establishing a rule of perfect peace and justice when war, like every other manifestation and consequence of sin, will be abolished. In the meantime, we live as peacemakers in the light and hope of that victory, calling the world to repentance and restoration, certain that those who work for peace and justice, for an affirmation of life in all its fullness, are on the winning side in history.

The Christian gospel therefore provides a compelling account of war. It accounts for its occurrence without justifying its existence or understating its seriousness. It underlines that it is a horror that we should not endure but for which we must bear responsibility. It points to its ultimate solution, without resorting to naive optimism in human institutions and ideas to abolish it, or a pessimism that causes us to give up hope and perpetuate its suffering by resigning ourselves to its inevitability. The gospel really is "good news" (the literal meaning of gospel), good news that the world needs to hear.

THE TASK OF THE CHURCH

As Bishop Bell reminded us during World War II, there is not a separate gospel for wartime and for peacetime. The task of the Christian in the War on Terror, as at every other time, is clear. Through it we can fulfill our true purpose which is, in the words of the Westminster Confession's Shorter Catechism, to "glorify God and enjoy him forever." How do we do this? We should constantly and prayerfully read and seek to understand the Bible, making Scripture our primary guide for understanding the times. We should reflect on the horror of war, which makes us alive to the reality of sin and humanity's need for the gospel. We should be filled with praise for the wonders of God's salvation, and cry out for the world to know it. We should glorify his rule as the only one that will last forever. This should lead us to devote all our energy to proclaiming the gospel to the world, calling it to repentance and true life, and working as peacemakers. It should fill us with hope, and encourage us to speak this hope and comfort to the world. It is vital to remember that we do this not as individuals but as "citizens of heaven," the church—a new nation made up of people called out of every nation. The church is God's demonstration to the world of the glorious salvation that he achieved at Calvary. As this new transnational nation of peacemakers, we show that the divisions of nationalism and the wounds of the past can and will be healed.

Bishop Bell's declaration that in wartime "it is the function of the Church at all costs to remain the Church" (see p. 20) can be thought about in terms of citizenship. As Christians we have at least two citizenships—we are citizens of heaven, and we are citizens of an earthly country. We must live responsibly as citizens of earthly states, honoring their leaders and laws as far as conscience allows, and seeking their peace and prosperity. Nonetheless, our primary allegiance is as citizens of heaven, to a different nation, homeland, code of living and head of state. When the church takes that to heart, it can transform the world, as examples in this book have shown.

However, when the church gets that allegiance the wrong way around, the consequences are often disastrous. It contributes to the problems of the world rather than alleviates them. In biblical language, it "loses it saltiness" and is "no longer good for anything, except to be thrown out and trampled" (Matthew 5:13). The church is particularly susceptible to making that mistake during wartime, and it is an error that we should be especially alert to in the charged emotions of the War on Terror. As Christians, our primary loyalty is to the kingdom of heaven, which in the current conflict includes fellow citizens from America, Britain, Iraq, Israel, Palestine and other nations, including secret believers in countries such as Afghanistan and Uzbekistan. When the church does not genuinely grasp that, passionately believe it and resolutely live it out, it fails in its calling to remain the church and brings shame, not honor, to its Lord.

CITIZENS OF HEAVEN

What it means to follow our Lord's call to be peacemakers as citizens of heaven in a particular context, such as the War on Terror, is open to different interpretations. That is important to underline. In the wisdom of God, Christianity does not espouse a single blueprint for organizing society, a uniform way of relating to political and legal structures. That would be contrary to the nature and function of the church as instituted by God. Indeed, when Christians (or, for that matter, followers of other religions) have tried to set up and enforce such systems, they are invariably harmful to true spirituality. Rather, as "salt and light," different groups of Christians in different times and places have found different ways of doing that. This book has given many rich examples. These include church leaders doing behind-the-scenes diplomatic work to orchestrate meetings between the representatives of rival or warring nations. They include individual congregations standing faithful to the gospel under brutal tyrants, or networks of Christians breaking the laws of their country to shield refugees; bereaved parents calling for forgiveness; and activists or missionaries placing themselves in dangerous situations to defuse violent tensions, protect the innocent and preach the gospel. It is important that the church make room for these very different ministries, so long as they are rooted in biblical truth, conducted under the guidance of the Spirit, and undertaken for the glory of God and the good of his creation.

The first thing the church needs to do in deciding how to respond to the War on Terror is to remember exactly what the church is, and recover a clear and passionate conviction of the truth of the basic Christian gospel. This book has aimed to assist this. By giving examples of how Christians at different times and places have worked this out, it has tried to show what might be possible in the current conflict. This is not to say that discussions around the politics of the War on Terror, historic church debates about war and specific recommendations on the current conflict are unnecessary. On the contrary, they are very important for any Christian trying to engage with the world, but only once we have established the basics. For this reason, three study guides have been included, each one addressing one of these topics. They also contain suggestions for further reading and ways individuals and churches can practically take this further.

No war, not least the War on Terror, is an easy time for most people to live through. We may suffer greatly, live in fear, and be overwhelmed by sorrow and anger. As Christians, we may forget our primary identity and allegiance as citizens of heaven. However, at the same time, war is a stark reminder of the truths of the gospel, which alone holds out ultimate hope for humankind. It obliges us to grow in faith in our Lord by stepping out in trust beyond natural ways of living and thinking. It enables us to proclaim the Christian hope in words and actions to a needy and unusually alert world. Are we ready for that challenge?

DIGGING DEEPER

THREE STUDY GUIDES

Exploring Terrorism and the War on Terror

DEFINING TERRORISM

Richard Falk, a professor of law at Princeton University, observes that the word *terrorism* first emerged as applied to the activities of the French revolutionary government, which used violence against civilian society to terrorize the population into acquiescing to the new government. More recently, the United States has backed groups like the Nicaraguan Contras in the 1980s, who sought to destabilize the left-wing Sandinista government by murdering civilians and creating mayhem in the state. Both of these examples, he argues, should properly be called terrorism. Thus it is confusing and dishonest for the U.S. government to declare a War on Terror, but also misleading to argue that terrorism's roots are in poverty, because political violence may emanate from the deepest recesses of government bureaucracy. He thus defines terrorism as "any type of political violence that lacks an adequate moral and legal justification, regardless of whether the actor is a revolutionary group or a government."

Martha Crenshaw, a professor at Wesleyan University, accepts that deprivation may be a *precondition* for terrorism in some circumstances, but not in all. She cites the example of militant left-wing groups in West Germany, Japan and Italy in the 1970s who attacked high-profile people and buildings they saw as representing the capitalist state. The terrorists were not downtrodden and poor but were from privileged backgrounds. However, while such terrorism is the result of "elite disaffection," a common *precipitant* (or immediate cause) may well be excessive government force. Thus, the British government's execution of the heroes of the Easter Rising against British rule in Ireland in 1916 set the stage for the emergence of the IRA. Crenshaw defines terrorism as "the premeditated use or threat of symbolic, low-level violence by conspiratorial organizations for purposes of political change." By "low-level" she does not mean insignificant or relatively harmless, but is referring to technology employed. This is typically in the form of relatively small and cheap explosives or hand-held guns and rockets, in contrast to heavy armor, artillery, warships, airplanes, helicopters, cruise missiles and other expensive weaponry that is generally the preserve of states.

Paul Wilkinson, a professor of international relations at St. Andrews University, sees the popular images of terrorism as insufficient when confronted with the vast and varied array of terrorist campaigns in history. Largely secular terrorism includes left-wing groups such as the Japanese Red Army, believed to be based in Lebanon, which attacks worldwide targets associated with "imperialism," and right-wing groups such as that which bombed the Alfred P. Murrah Federal Building in Oklahoma in 1995, killing nearly two hundred people. Ethnic separatist desires for an independent homeland, such as the Basques of Spain or the Republicans of Northern Ireland, remain the most frequent motivations behind terrorist actions. Terror has also been a weapon of religiously inspired political campaigns, from the Jewish Sicarii who waged a campaign of assassination against the Romans and those who collaborated with them in first-century Palestine, to modern Islamist groups. He identifies state terror as the most lethal, typified by the former Soviet

Union, Iran's backing of anti-Israeli groups like Hezbollah, and Israel's campaign of extrajudicial killings and assassinations of Palestinian opponents. He thus defines terrorism as

the systematic use of coercive intimidation, usually to service political ends. It is used to create and exploit a climate of fear among a wider target group than the immediate victims of the violence, often to publicise a cause, as well as to coerce a target into acceding to terrorist aims. . . . It can be employed by desperate and weak minorities, by states as a tool of domestic and foreign policy, or by belligerents as an accompaniment or additional weapon in all types and stages of warfare.

Wilkinson's definition is a good one, because it attempts to encompass as many different facets of contemporary terrorism as possible. However, not everyone would agree with him, and it is a notoriously difficult term to define. Indeed, the United Nations member states have not been able to agree on a single definition of the word. This is partially because the definition used helps determine the type of response suggested, and this itself is often revealing of personal political commitments. It is important to bear that in mind as we turn to the next section.

FIVE PERSPECTIVES ON THE WAR ON TERROR

Moral-patriotic. Charles Kegley, a professor of international relations at the University of South Carolina, defines terrorism as "violence or the threat of violence undertaken to create alarm and fear," and by this token he identifies Osama bin Laden as the arch terrorist, who gloated after 9/11 that "America is full of fear. . . . Nobody in the United States will feel safe." Whereas once terrorism was a tactic to attract attention to a cause by killing a small number of people, 9/11 ushered in a "new age" of mass killing with new rules of violence. This terrorism is "a sadistic assault on the principles and political culture of the United States and its allies—on their very way of life." The motivation is pure evil, as the terrorists' only desire is "to make the target suffer for what the target is, what it does, and the values for which the target stands." Thus it can in no way be understood in political or historical terms, but is rather an attack on American values and lifestyles, indeed, directed against all "peace-loving people on the planet." This being so, terrorism is "a disease highly resistant to control." As Kegley sees terrorism as "acts that cannot be deterred or prevented through negotiated compromise," it is clear that an uncompromising military response is necessary.

Political. The War on Terror as a moral explanation advanced above has come in for sharp criticism from all sectors of society. One source of such criticism comes from experts who analyze al-Qaeda as a political phenomenon. A prime example of this category is Michael Scheuer, who served in the Central Intelligence Agency for twenty-two years, including as chief of the bin Laden unit at the Counterterrorist Center. In 2004 he published anonymously a book entitled *Imperial Hubris: Why the West Is Losing the War on Terror.* It is a searing attack on the War on Terror and the attitude of recent U.S. presidents, policymakers and media elites to Osama bin Laden. He considers bin Laden neither a lunatic nor an evildoer motivated by the desire to destroy America, and he believes that those in the United States who push this account, and who believe that only a minority of extremists would oppose the U.S. role in the world, are dangerously misguided. Instead, Scheuer considers his enemy to be a "truly remarkable man." His political demands are clear, focused and limited foreign policy objectives: essentially, the removal of U.S. troops from Muslim lands, the end of Western protection of repressive Muslim regimes, and the termination of U.S. support for the oppression of Muslims by Israel and some other states such as Russia. Scheuer reckons that bin Laden conceives of his struggle not as terrorism, but as a defensive war against foreign aggressors. bin Laden's brilliance, according to Scheuer, is that he has combined powerful nationalist and religious ideologies into a coherent and consistent program that resonates with large numbers of Muslims, even though most do not support his methods.

Scheuer argues that Washington elites have not understood this, refusing to pursue bin Laden in the early 1990s when his danger was apparent. Instead, the hopelessly miscalculated wars on Afghanistan and Iraq have not only failed to break al-Qaeda, but have provided demonstrations of the kinds of abuses that bin Laden accuses the U.S. of doing. The U.S. is thus completing the radicalization of the Islamic world that bin Laden himself was unable to achieve, and therefore, argues Scheuer, "the United States of America remains bin Laden's only indispensable ally." Al-Qaeda is preparing for a long war to break down the political and economic will of Washington to maintain costly occupations, and without massive amounts of force and money, the U.S. will eventually be obliged to withdraw from the region and end support of Israel. What is needed, insists Scheuer, is not the pride of assuming that we are winning against al-Qaeda, but serious and decisive military action, not half-hearted and botched attempts like the Afghanistan intervention, and foolish enterprises like the Iraq invasion.

Another political explanation of the War on Terror is provided by Robert Pape, a political scientist at the University of Chicago. His analysis arises from a study of suicide terrorism in general. He has compiled an extensive list of all terrorist suicide bombings from 1980 to 2003. He concludes that the vast majority are intended to compel democracies to withdraw military forces from territory that the terrorists consider to be their homeland. Religion is rarely the root cause, although it is used by organizations in recruiting. Nearly all the attacks occurred as part of organized campaigns against democracies seen to be weak. Around half of the eighteen campaigns he identified during this time could be judged partially or wholly successful.

He believes that al-Qaeda's campaign against the United States fits this pattern of a political nationalist movement. Osama bin Laden has spoken repeatedly about expelling U.S. forces from Muslim lands and reducing U.S. power in the Middle East, using religion to strengthen his case. Most al-Qaeda recruits are from countries with a strong U.S. military presence or alliance. The U.S. invasion of Iraq in 2003 triggered a new al-Qaeda campaign, which has drawn many more recruits. To defeat al-Qaeda, Pape suggests, military occupation to remake society is counterproductive, and compromise is not feasible. Rather, to maintain U.S. oil interests, Pape recommends that the United States gradually withdraw all its forces from the Middle East, and rely instead on alliances with states that it could use to bring troops in at short notice if emergencies arise.

Historical-political. A different approach to the moral or political explanations of 9/11 endorsed by supporters or radical opponents of President Bush is offered by historians of U.S. foreign policy. The best known of these is found in *Blowback* by Chalmers Johnson of the University of California, San Diego. "Blowback" is a term from the battlefields of World War I, when artillery gunners effectively killed their own soldiers as poison gas fired at the enemy was blown back at them by the wind. It has come to mean the unintended harmful consequences of secret intelligence programs. Johnson traces the relationship of the United States to bin Laden's al-Qaeda network. To fight Soviet Union forces that had invaded Afghanistan in 1979, the

Central Intelligence Agency secretly collaborated with Pakistan to fund and arm mujahideen Islamist resistance, including bin Laden himself, from 1984 onward (incidentally, the British SAS helped to train some of these fighters). Bin Laden broke with the U.S. when it reneged on its apparent commitment to withdraw its forces from Saudi Arabia once Iraq had been expelled from Kuwait in 1991. Bin Laden was angry that "heathen" troops should occupy his homeland where Islam's holy cities of Mecca and Medina are located. When Islamists almost succeeded in blowing up the World Trade Center in 1993, explosive manuals supplied by the CIA were found in their possession.

John Cooley traces this "blowback" to other countries. With the defeat of the Soviet Union, thousands of Muslims from around the world who fought in the U.S.-backed mujahideen had been imbued with radical ideology, military experience and optimism. They returned home to foment Islamist violence in Chechnya, Bosnia, Saudi Arabia, Southeast Asia, China, Algeria and elsewhere. In the preface to the 2004 edition of Johnson's *Blowback* he reminded readers that in the 2000 edition he had argued that "many aspects of what the American government had done abroad virtually invited retaliatory attacks"; Johnson saw in 9/11 the grim realization of that prediction. He criticized President Bush's statement on the day of the plane hijackings that America had been attacked by motiveless "evildoers" because it was "a beacon of freedom." Rather, he insisted, "The suicidal assassins of September 11, 2001, did not 'attack America,' as political leaders and news media in the United States have tried to maintain; they attacked American foreign policy."

In this sense, bin Laden's attacks can be seen as part of a multipronged effort to compel the United States to disengage from majority-Muslim lands. It is not entirely far-fetched to see this as a military strategy that could potentially succeed. After all, the U.S.

withdrew from Lebanon following the devastating suicide bombing of a marine barracks in 1983, and from Somalia a decade later
when al-Qaeda-linked forces inflicted losses on U.S. troops. Martha Crenshaw observes that in a war of attrition, such as the War
on Terror, the side with the superior motivation and endurance may
win.

Unlike some extreme commentators, these historical accounts
do not blame the United States for the 9/11 attacks. Moral responsibility for the atrocities must rest with those who planned and carried them out. They do, however, argue that they could only occur
in the context of certain significant U.S. foreign policy decisions,
and may thus be taken as implying that those lessons need to be
learned in order to prevent a repetition.

Economic. One radical answer to the question, "What was September 11 about?" comes from the pens of four San Francisco Bay
intellectuals who write under the collective name "Retort." Drawing on a strand of 1960s Marxist thought, they suggest that the
world is suffering from the "nightmare" of "internal colonization"
by capitalism. By this, they mean that every part of our lives has
been taken over by rampant capitalism as propagated through the
media. This has produced an atomized society of mindless consum-
ers unable to resist the sterilization of their lives by capitalism.
Within the Islamic world, the misuse of oil dollars to enrich corrupt, secular nationalist dictators and the impoverishment of general society following economic collapse in the early 1980s showed
the bankruptcy of the West. This left radical Islam as the only viable
alternative to Western-backed local despots.

Retort then posit that the suicide bombers of September 11, reacting against this, knew that they were too weak seriously to dis-
rupt flows of capital, so they went instead for a "spectacle," their
primary aim being to create an image that showed the U.S. empire

as weak. The U.S., they argue, has not known how to respond—it cannot deny the news footage of the Twin Towers collapsing that has been seen all over the world, so has acted like an enraged beast in projects like the botched attempts at colonizing Afghanistan and Iraq. While factors such as oil and grand strategic plans are important, the War on Terror is a struggle over images and spectacles.

A more coherent and hard-hitting critique of the War on Terror is provided by Jewish-American academic Noam Chomsky, described by the *New York Times* as "arguably the most important intellectual alive." Over many decades, Chomsky has sustained a critique of U.S. foreign policy as being primarily about the promotion of U.S. economic interests that is justified by misleading moral claims managed by an efficient propaganda machine. He cites numerous instances of U.S. open and hidden military interventions around the world since World War II in attempts to affect the internal politics of states and ensure that their policies favored U.S. business. Because this has often involved overthrowing democratic governments or backing brutal dictators, Chomsky argues that U.S. foreign policy cannot be essentially about promoting the spread of democracy. He also contends that such foreign policy can continue due to amnesia created by the consistent failure of the media to reveal the full truth to the American public, a situation engineered by sophisticated techniques of media manipulation.

Chomsky believes that, far from being something new, the War on Terror is no real departure from this story of U.S. economic might dressed in moral rhetoric, in this case about defeating terrorism, reducing dangerous weapons, promoting democracy and protecting the innocent. Chomsky marshals a vast array of evidence, including formal statements and candid quotations by U.S. government and exgovernmental officials to support his argument. He denies that the War on Terror is about defeating terrorism, observing that the inva-

sions of Afghanistan and Iraq have reinvigorated violent Islamist
networks and led to unprecedented numbers of retaliatory Islamist
attacks, just as many experts warned would happen. He also contends that the U.S. itself shelters terrorists from wars it has backed
in Latin America. Neither is it to protect the world from "weapons
of mass destruction," as no one seriously believed that Iraq presented a threat to the world, and the successful activities of UN
weapons inspectors in Iraq were curtailed by President Bush, who
has also squashed international attempts to limit the development of
chemical weapons. Nor does he believe that President Bush is really
committed to promoting democracy in the Muslim world, as evidenced by the unsavory alliances with repressive Muslim dictatorships from Pakistan and Uzbekistan to Saudi Arabia and Algeria.
Finally, he is scornful of U.S. declarations that it is committed to protecting innocent life. He argues that far more civilians died as a result
of U.S. bombing in Afghanistan and Iraq than perished in the Twin
Towers, and that the United States has hampered attempts to widen
medicine distribution in Africa that would save large numbers of
lives but harm the profits of the U.S. pharmaceutical industry.

Rather, argues Chomsky, the War on Terror is part of what he
calls an "imperial grand strategy" to further the same old national
interests. He observes that Bush insiders have confirmed that the
administration had already been seeking to conquer Iraq before
September 2001, and argues that the al-Qaeda attacks provided the
desired opportunity. In particular, he cites the U.S. government
document National Security Strategy published in 2002. This outlined a concept whereby the United States would take preemptive
action to prevent any potentially hostile rival equaling its power,
and would use this position of domination to institute a world of
free-market economics and democracy. Chomsky observes that this
right may only be appropriated by the United States and its desig-

nated allies. In effect, argues Chomsky, this is a blatant statement of perpetual U.S. imperialism, which is what the War on Terror is really about.

Conservative. Criticism of the War on Terror has not been confined to left-wing radicals such as Retort and Chomsky; far from it, its most vocal opponents have included conservatives who have previously served under right-wing U.S. presidents or in the military. They turn their guns on the "neoconservatives," a group who believe that America should take an aggressive military and political strategy over the coming years to force nondemocratic regimes to adopt American economic and political values. According to this critique, these ideologues coalesced around a group formed in 1997 called the Project for the New American Century, which campaigned for massive increases in U.S. military expenditure to fund an aggressive foreign policy to remake the world in a way more amenable to America and democracy—beginning with the invasion of Iraq. Their moment came with the election of George W. Bush in 2000, when they were able to manipulate a relatively weak and inexperienced president to capture U.S. foreign policy. This critique is advanced forcibly by self-identified conservatives Stefan Halper (who served under Presidents Nixon and Reagan) and Jonathan Clarke (member of a right-wing think tank). Unlike radical critiques, they share with neoconservatives a belief that America is an immense force for good in the world, but they part company with the neoconservative belief that the best way to project American values in the world is through unilateral force to overthrow hostile regimes and set up democracies. Halper and Clarke argue that the War on Terror has damaged democracy at home, militarized society, alienated allies abroad, and created new enemies and terrorists hostile to America across the world. They conclude that this War on Terror has made the world more dangerous, not less—a process even more sinister because it depends on the manipulation of fear and danger.

Richard Clarke, another former official and the top professional expert on terrorism under four U.S. presidents, has launched a similar broadside against his old boss. On September 12, 2001, President Bush met with Clarke and other advisers and told them, "See if Saddam did this. See if he's linked in any way." Clarke and others were incredulous, as they knew that there were no links with Iraq, but Bush kept insisting. Clarke puts this down as the neoconservative drive to invade Iraq, justified to the public by administration of false claims that Iraq was connected to 9/11 and that it had "weapons of mass destruction," claims derived from phony evidence from Iraqi defectors that it had paid.

With the benefit of further hindsight, this critique of the War on Terror has been restated by *New York Times* journalist Michael Gordon and Marine Corps lieutenant general Bernard Trainor in their book *Cobra II: The Inside Story of the Invasion and Occupation of Iraq*. They argue that the neoconservatives saw 9/11 as a golden opportunity to put their doctrine into action, in the form of the War on Terror. Central to this was the invasion of Iraq. Claims that Iraq was a threat to America were clearly ludicrous, but were a pretext for two major aims. The first was to reform the domestic U.S. structures of decision-making, increasing the power of the president and the Pentagon to make war at the expense of more naturally cautious bodies such as the Joint Chiefs of Staff, Congress, the judiciary and the CIA. This was to facilitate the second aim, the aggressive and proactive remaking of the oil-rich Middle East along pro-American lines. Central to this would be the construction of a "friendly" democratic Iraq. This would reduce U.S. reliance on Saudi Arabia, an increasingly problematic ally given that most of the 9/11 hijackers, not to mention Osama bin Laden, were Saudis. It would also act as a launch pad to threaten or invade neighboring states such as Iran and Syria, and a model of democratic capitalist development in the region. The ultimate strategic goal was to eliminate the conditions that bred and sustained violent Islamic radicalism. The foolishness, arrogance and incompetence of President Bush's War on Terror as plotted by the neoconservatives has, conservative critics argue, actually set back the struggle against radical Islamists.

CONCLUSION

The different positions presented here are not exhaustive but are summarized to give an idea of the variety of reactions to the September 11 attacks and to President Bush's policy response to them. These analyses widely diverge, both on *why* the September 11 attacks occurred and *whether* the War on Terror was the correct response. These divergences did not remain in the realm of intellectual ideas. Indeed, from massive street demonstrations across the world to fierce political and judicial battles in the United States and allied nations, the War on Terror has become the hottest political struggle for years in countries such as the U.S. and the U.K.

Nonetheless, in spite of these battles, the commentators outlined above can be said to agree generally on three things. These are that radical Islamist violence is a threat that needs addressing, that this must involve changing U.S. foreign policy and that mistakes were made that contributed to the events leading to the 9/11 attacks. Left-wingers may suggest that Islamist violence needs addressing by dealing with poverty and dissatisfaction, and that U.S. foreign policy has exacerbated the anger and should be radically reconsidered. Right-wingers may argue that violent Islamism needs addressing by more force, and by pruning the internal bureaucracies and laws that hamper the United States in its war. Those on the left may argue that U.S. foreign policy, driven by self-interest, has been largely a force for bad in the world, whereas those on the right would insist that, on balance, it is a force for good, as America embodies noble values: both sides, nonetheless, want it to be a force for good. These three points of agreement, together with the political differences behind different conclusions, find their counterparts in Christian responses to the War on Terror, as we will see in Study Guide 3. Before that, however, it is necessary to look at how Christians have traditionally addressed the question of war, as this background was the other major factor molding Christian responses. That is the topic of the second study guide.

FOR FURTHER STUDY

Terrorism

Charles Kegley, ed., *The New Global Terrorism: Characteristics, Causes, Controls* (Upper Saddle River, N.J.: Prentice Hall, 2003). This is an accessible introduction to the study of terrorism, containing many short chapters on the causes, types, consequences and responses to terrorism, and written by various authors, including Falk, Crenshaw and Wilkinson (discussed above). Politically, the book tends to be more conservative.

Group study. In the book of Jeremiah, the prophet frequently uses the word *terror* in prophesying about the calamities that will befall the Jews, their leaders and neighboring states as a result of sin. Briefly summarize to the group the definitions of *terrorism* provided in this study guide (see "Defining terrorism" on pp. 139-41). Then, using a concordance, look up every reference to the word *terror* in the book of Jeremiah. Compare Jeremiah's idea of terror and terrorism with those discussed in this section.

Perspectives on the War on Terror

Moral-patriotic. President George W. Bush's "Address to a Joint Session of Congress and the American People," September 20, 2001, and "State of the Union Address," January 30, 2002, are available at http://www.whitehouse.gov. Charles Kegley's support for the president is contained in his essay in the book mentioned above.

Political. Michael Scheuer, *Imperial Hubris: Why the West Is Losing the War on Terror* (Washington, D.C.: Brassey's Inc., 2004), first released anonymously; Robert Pape, *Dying to Win: The Strategic Logic of Suicide Terrorism* (New York: Random House, 2005).

Historical-political. Chalmers Johnson, *Blowback: The Costs and Consequences of American Empire,* 2nd ed. (New York: Henry Holt, 2004); John Cooley, *Unholy Wars: Afghanistan, America, and International Terrorism* (London: Pluto Press, 2002).

Economic. Retort's book, *Afflicted Powers: Capital and Spectacle in a New Age of War* (London: Verso, 2004); an article-length version published the same year with the same title can be found in the journal *New Left Review* 27 (May-June 2004): 5-21; Noam Chomsky, *Hegemony or Survival: America's Quest for Global Dominance* (London: Penguin, 2004).

Conservative. Stefan Halper and Jonathan Clarke, *America Alone: The Neo-Conservatives and the Global Order* (Cambridge: Cambridge University Press, 2004); Richard Clarke, *Against All Enemies: Inside America's War on Terror* (New York: Free Press, 2004); Michael Gordon and Bernard Trainor, *Cobra II: The Inside Story of the Invasion and Occupation of Iraq* (London: Atlantic Books, 2006).

Christian Stances on War

The first study guide explored how various political writers have tried to explain and respond to the War on Terror. The third study guide will look at specific Christian responses to it. This second study guide is a bridge between the two, looking at how Christians have responded to the question of war in general. Anyone who reads the daily newspapers regularly encounters the word *war,* from violent "wars" between states, gangs, and governments and terrorists, to metaphorical "wars" against AIDS, corruption and the waste of water in the home. This can add to the confusion surrounding the word. What, exactly, does *war* mean?

War is not the same thing as a fight between individuals or a spontaneous violent clash between groups such as gangs. Rather, as one dictionary defines it, war is a state of "armed, often prolonged conflict carried on between nations, states or parties." That is to say, it is a social practice, often involving considerable resources of organization, money, logistics, manpower and information, sustained over a period of many months or years. Animals regularly *fight,* but (with the possible exception of ants) only humans organize *wars.* Because war can be so destructive, Christians have given much thought about how we should respond to it. Four general schools of thought can be identified: holy war, realism, just-war theory and pacifism.

"HOLY WAR" AND "REALISM"

"Holy war" sees war as good in itself, because it fosters Christian virtues such as loyalty and endurance, brings unity to the church by channeling energies against an external foe, and, most of all, brings glory to God by destroying his foes. For example, a crusader wrote of the slaughter of civilians in Jerusalem in 1099 that

> wonderful sights were to be seen. Some of our men cut off the heads of their enemies; others shot them with arrows, so that they fell from the towers, others tortured them longer by casting them into the flames. . . . [I]t was a just and splendid judgement of God that this place should be filled with the blood of unbelievers.

Holy war leans heavily upon a literal application of portions of the Old Testament, such as the book of Joshua. Although elements of this tradition persist in some quarters of the U.S. military, evangelicals mostly dismiss it because of its failure to account properly for the culmination of the old covenant in the gospel, since the people of God (the church) are no longer a territorial nation as Old Testament Israel was.

"Realism" sees war as a form of politics, a way of extending the power of one state at the expense of another. Because it is one of the basic ways that states relate to one another in a world with no higher authority, realism considers it futile to try to regulate it. Realism considers it not only pointless but positively dangerous to subject war to moral reflection. According to this reasoning, for example, if a soldier is fighting to capture disputed oil-rich territory, he sees his enemy as a fellow soldier struggling for the same goal and is unlikely to bear him personal animosity. However, if he considers his war to have moral justification, for example, to be divinely ordained in pursuit of justice or a humanitarian mission to rescue needy people, then he must regard his opponent as less moral than himself for opposing this, and he is thus likely to be more destructive and vindictive. Evangelical Christians generally reject realism, insisting that all human activities fall under the sovereignty of God and must be judged by his holy law.

Both holy war and realism are largely rejected by contemporary Christian thinkers, so we will focus instead on the two main schools of thought among modern evangelicals, "just-war theory" and "pacifism." Although they are generally placed as extreme opposites, they have a great deal in common. Both reject the celebration of violence in holy war, seeing war as evil and an aberration from God's plan and will for humanity, which is peace and plenty (or "shalom"). Both reject the amorality of realism, insisting that every human activity is subject to the ethical scrutiny of God's will as revealed in the Bible. Where they part company is their position on war in the age of the gospel, that interim period between the death and resurrection of Christ and his return in glory when his final rule of peace and justice will be fully established. Just-war theorists contend that the Bible authorizes Christians to engage in war instigated by legitimate authorities established by God for the purpose of promoting justice and peace. Pacifists contend that it does not, and that believers must find nonviolent ways to follow Christ's call to be peacemakers. It is to these two traditions that we will now turn.

JUST-WAR THEORY

The rise and development of just-war theory. Anthropologists have shown that not all human societies have developed or employed war, but those that have tend to develop codes to regulate its conduct. The most important such code developed in Europe is known as "just-war theory."

Just-war theory draws on a variety of cultural influences. Its foundation was laid by Greek and Roman thinkers such as Aristotle and Cicero, who discussed just causes for war and the necessary authority to declare it. The later Roman Christian leaders Ambrose and Augustine adopted this and adapted it to Christianity, adding that wars must be fought with the right intention (Christian love, not vengeance or greed). From medieval codes of chivalry came laws about just conduct in warfare, and the protection of noncombatants. There was no smooth development, and at times just-war theory fell out of fashion almost completely, but by the fifteenth century these often-contradictory ideas from multiple sources had come together into a broadly recognizable form.

From the sixteenth century the development of just-war theory was largely carried forward by secular thinkers, eventually morphing into modern international laws on war, such as the Geneva Conventions. Even though it has traditionally been mainly a Roman Catholic doctrine, its premise is still assumed by many other major Christian denominations today. Indeed, Charles Reed, an influential thinker in the Anglican church and author of a recent book on the subject, has argued that a recovery of just-war theory should be the basis of the church's engagement with the state on issues of international conflict.

At its best, just-war theory is about continual ethical reflection on the morality of a war, and is not a set of boxes that a politician can check to establish if a war is "just." Nevertheless, it traditionally distinguishes between two sets of rules. The first concerns "just resort to war" (*jus ad bellum* in Latin) to establish the criteria by which a war may be begun. Five criteria are commonly advanced. The war must have a *just cause*, that is, self-defense against an unlawful attack, or the righting of wrong and the reestablishment of peace. A just cause would not include seizing territory or natural resources. Second, it must be waged by a *right authority*. A group of people such as criminals, rebels, or community or private militias cannot band together and start a war on their own initiative, even if the cause is just. In modern states, the established government acting in self-defense, or the United Nations Security Council, are regarded as the only right authorities. Third, the proper authority must have a *right intention*. It is one thing to identify a just cause such as resisting the invasion of an ally, but if the authority is only using that as a mask for the real purpose of securing access to natural resources, for example, then the intention is not just. Likewise, vengeance is not a just intention. Fourth, there must be a *reasonable chance of success*. Even if the intent is just, it is not just to launch a war that has little chance of succeeding, as the expected good results of the war must outweigh the evil of war, that is, the suffering that it brings to all involved. Finally, war must be launched as a *last resort*, when all other avenues of resolving the conflict have been exhausted.

The second set of criteria is known as *jus in bello* ("just conduct in war"), and concerns the actual conduct of war once it has begun. Two requirements are commonly stipulated in this category. The first is *discrimination* between legitimate and illegitimate targets. Thus civilians and noncombatants such as medical personnel and chaplains are not to be deliberately targeted for attack, although if they are killed as the indirect result of an attack on a military target, then that is not regarded as a crime. Likewise, prisoners of war must not be executed or otherwise ill-treated. Second, force used must be *proportional* to the aim, and only that firepower strictly necessary to secure one's objective must be used—even against military personnel.

Just-war theory is a dynamic and evolving tradition, and some thinkers have recently proposed the addition of a third category to these two traditional ones, *jus post bellum,* or "justice after war." By this count, a war can only be considered just if the victors put sufficient planning and effort into stabilizing the situation and restoring order and well being after any war. Some writers have suggested that this must involve installing functioning democracies. It should be apparent that these criteria are highly demanding. Even if a war has been begun justly, it may subsequently become unjust by virtue of the way it is fought. Far from celebrating it, the firm presumption of just-war theory is against war: "History knows of no just wars," writes just-war theorist and theologian Oliver O'Donovan. It is formulated to aid statesmen and women in practical reasoning in the murkiness and confusion of the real world by giving a moral framework for reflecting on different aspects of war, and to enable the church to counsel governments over the wisdom of their actions.

Just-war theory—seven debates and controversies. Unsurprisingly, just-war theory has generated enormous controversy in its history, and for many reasons. First, many people have argued that the technology of modern warfare has undermined just-war reasoning. How could a nuclear war of annihilation, for example, conceivably be "just"? Likewise, the shift away from traditional wars between the armies of states to nonstate terrorist insurgency and civil wars of ethnic genocide has led many people to question the usefulness of a theory that is heavily tied to the state. However, it should be noted that just-war theory is not a single, unchangeable system but is dynamic and has traditionally responded to new developments—as it has to these.

The most common debate concerns the objectivity of just-war theory. Advocates argue that it provides an objective framework that can be applied evenly to any conflict by any belligerent. Critics observe that its advocates are generally politically centrist or con-

servative supporters of the wars of their states, a tendency that has
been marked in theological debate on the War on Terror. However,
even if this is the case, it does not therefore follow that the theory
is invalid. The major difficulty arises because the theory's criteria
inevitably involve answering questions such as "does Iraq *really*
possess weapons that present a danger?" (just cause); "isn't it just
'all about oil'?" (right intention); and "wouldn't United Nations
sanctions work given long enough?" (last resort). These are not legal questions but political judgments informed by how much one
trusts certain governments. As it would be impossible to expect
agreement on them, this objection may be misplaced.

This has informed a third criticism of just-war theory: that it is
a cynical (or naive) device to allow the powerful to legitimize their
wars. While this has often happened, advocates argue that this is a
misunderstanding. The whole thrust of just-war theory is to reduce
both the frequency and destructiveness of wars. Most scholarly advocates of just-war theory sincerely believe war to be a regrettable
evil, but one that is necessary for the pursuit of peace and justice in
a fallen world. Accepting that human security is more frequently
threatened than protected by military force, Patrick Hayden asserts
from a just-war view that "a just war is not to be regarded as a
good thing *per se* but as the lesser of two evils."

This nonetheless leads to a paradox—can a good world be built
on something accepted, however regrettably, as evil? This fourth
criticism is one of the major arguments advanced against just-war
theory—not that it is sometimes used to justify a particular war, but
that it provides a general moral endorsement of war as an accept-
able element of international society. However humble and critical
it might be, it still ends up sustaining the system of war and is thus
a major obstacle to peace. In reply, just-war theorists must repeat
that they sincerely regret the occurrence of war but believe, on bal-

ance, it is necessary in order to prevent greater evils.

This tension lies at the heart of the debate of most concern to evangelical Christians: just how biblical is just-war theory? Even most of its advocates accept that it cannot be easily read from Scripture and fits uneasily with either the apparent holy-war tradition of, say, Joshua, and the nonviolence of Christ and the apostles. Church tradition, especially the voluminous writing of luminaries such as Augustine and Aquinas, is generally a more important reference point for just-war theorists than the Bible. Indeed, advocates can point to very few texts to support it, and whole books on it generally contain only a smattering of biblical references, often removed from their contexts. Charles Reed, mentioned above as an influential Anglican advocate, argues that the tradition "seeks to bridge the gap between the Old and New Testament." Evangelical critics of just-war theory would deny that there is any such "gap" between Old and New Testaments, and insist that the Bible is a higher authority than church tradition, especially church tradition with its roots in pagan thought and Roman Catholic theology.

A sixth area of debate regards the role of the church. Advocates of just-war theory contend that the lack of scriptural and spiritual language makes it easier for Christians to engage in important public debates in secular terms that do not immediately alienate non-Christians. While many of its advocates would accept that it is a lower ethic than that taught by Christ, they would argue that Christ's ethic was not meant to be applied literally to politics in this fallen world until he himself returns. They would also say that just-war theory is superior to most alternatives, and can arguably point to its role in informing international law; for example, nowadays most states feel obliged to spare civilians in war wherever possible, not execute captured soldiers, etc. However, critics would say that this is to miss the point: although it may be a higher ethic than many worldly ones, it is far lower than the ethic of Christ, and Christians are called to live out the teachings of Christ in obedient faith, not aim at what might humanly appear more reasonable.

A final criticism is a practical observation about evangelism and the reputation of the church. Proponents of this position assert that, cumulatively, throughout history the reputation of the church and the gospel has been damaged by wars that Christian thinkers of their age sincerely believed to be just, and argue that this is an indictment of the tradition in general. Nowadays, it is increasingly missionaries who make this point, as they experience American/ Western military foreign policies as a chief source of hostility to the gospel among unreached peoples, who often see Christianity and Western militarism as one and the same thing. Just-war theorists would say that this is regrettable but is a result of the misuse of the theory.

CHRISTIAN PACIFISM

Although most societies have developed some form of warfare, it is also the case that the fundamental legitimacy of its existence has frequently been questioned. Pacifism is the rejection of war as a means of resolving international disputes. This rejection may be based upon secular political grounds, such as the pragmatic calculation that war is ineffective. It may spring from a personal revulsion to violence, or a humanistic optimism that war will disappear as the human race evolves to become more civilized. Christian pacifism is the belief that God forbids participation in war.

There are a number of different types of Christian pacifism. For example, liberal versions may hold that nonviolence is a more effective and civilized way of resolving disputes than warfare is. The essence of evangelical Christian pacifism is different. It holds that

God, as revealed in the Bible, commands Christians not to engage in warfare. It is built on three main biblical justifications.

The first biblical basis of evangelical Christian pacifism is the theology of the covenant. This accepts that God commanded his people to engage in warfare in the Old Testament but contends that this was for a specific time and purpose that no longer applies. Because God's covenant community was a single people with a country, Israel, God allowed warfare in order to ensure their survival. The Israelites were to annihilate their enemies in the Promised Land to avoid being led astray by local practices of idol worship. Israel needed to survive because through it the Messiah would come at the climax of history. Although many expected that the Messiah, the "Son of David," would be a mighty warrior, God progressively revealed to the prophets that he would be the opposite: a "Prince of Peace," who would abolish "bow and sword and battle . . . from the land" (Hosea 2:18). Salvation would be achieved not by a glorious military leader but by the sufferings of God's servant, who would not fight his enemies but die for their justification (see Isaiah 9 and 53; Hosea 2). The law of Moses, including the laws on war, was appropriate for its time serving as a schoolmaster until the gospel age (Galatians 3). In Christ, the purpose of the Old Testament law was fulfilled. God's new covenant people, the church, are justified and sanctified by the Holy Spirit's application of the work of Christ in their lives, so they can now live among sinners yet remain holy. The age of war has thus ended for God's covenant community.

The second argument for evangelical Christian pacifism is the teaching and life of Christ. Jesus insisted that his followers should love their enemies, be peacemakers, bless those who curse them and not use violence when attacked. He put this into practice throughout his life and, most famously, at his death. His arrest and execution were a perfect example of his teaching—forbidding his

disciples to use the sword in defense, and loving his enemies by
praying for them as they tortured him on the cross. Bishop J. C.
Ryle said that "Christ is our pattern as well as our propitiation."
That means that his death not only won our salvation on Calvary,
but his life was a model for ours. In his Gospel account, John
records Jesus' commission to the church as, "Peace be with you! As
the Father has sent me, I am sending you" (John 20:21). Therefore,
Christian pacifists argue that we must obey Christ's commands of
nonviolent enemy love by imitating the life of love that he lived.

The third scriptural basis for Christian pacifism is apostolic
teaching and practice. This argument contends that the apostles
held the same position as Christ. Cited as evidence is Peter, who
wrote that "Christ suffered for you, leaving you an example, that
you should follow in his steps. . . . When they hurled their insults
at him, he did not retaliate; when he suffered, he made no threats"
(1 Peter 2:21-23). Paul also appears to back this up. He repudiated
his preconversion belief in violence to further God's kingdom by
persecuting his enemies, teaching "The weapons we fight with are
not the weapons of the world" (2 Corinthians 10:4). In his letter to
the Ephesians, he outlines his "gospel of peace": whereas humans
had been at enmity with God and other nations, Jesus "preached
peace" to Gentiles and Jews alike, uniting them in a new creation,
the church, a transnational body of peacemakers that displays
God's glory to "the rulers and authorities" (Ephesians 3:10). On
this basis, evangelical Christian pacifists argue that believers are
forbidden from harming their enemies in warfare, but must rather
devote their energy to preaching the gospel and building the
church, God's alternative version of renewed humanity.

Although Christian pacifists hold the Bible as more authoritative
than church teaching, they do not dismiss the latter. They point to
the recognition by most historians that Christian pacifism was the

norm for some centuries after Christ. There are many records of Christians being martyred for refusing to join or fight in the Roman army, and leaving the army was a precondition for baptism in early church codes of conduct. The church father Tertullian forbade Christian involvement in warfare because "If we are commanded to love our enemies, whom have we to hate? If injured, we are forbidden to retaliate. . . . Christ, in disarming Peter, unarmed every soldier." Christian pacifists suggest that the modeling of an attractive Christian life of peacemaking communities was a great evangelistic tool in that violent period. They contend that it was not until Christianity was co-opted and corrupted by Roman emperors in the fourth century that pacifism was abandoned. More recently, the modern evangelical mission movement to non-European peoples has informed evangelical Christian pacifism. The biographies of "heroes of the faith," who were opposed and sometimes killed by violent nonbelievers, have modeled nonviolent ways of responding to violence by trusting in the miraculous power of God.

There has been much disagreement among evangelical Christian pacifists on how believers should positively relate to the state and engage in international politics. Positions range from basically withdrawing from society to organizing mass attempts to prevent wars and overthrow unjust governments. However, evangelical Christian pacifists all agree that the Bible forbids believers from harming enemies by participating in warfare.

Christian pacifism—seven debates and controversies. As suggested above, Christian pacifism actually includes a variety of divergent positions, and has less internal coherence as a label than just-war theory. However, there are a range of criticisms that can be leveled at most variants of it.

One criticism of pacifism is that it relies on a handful of texts taken out of context, typically the Sermon on the Mount and Ro-

mans 12:9—13:7. It is argued that this is poor biblical exegesis, as
Scripture must be taken as a whole, and parts of it should not be
interpreted in opposition to others. Some variants of pacifism endorsed by liberals do indeed fall foul of this criticism. However, this
is an unfair characterization of evangelical versions of Christian
pacifism such as those outlined above, which generally make more
rigorous use of systematic biblical interpretation than just-war or
holy-war theories do.

A similar criticism of pacifism is that voiced by Charles Reed, who
says it "reflects an ideal of human nature, which fails to take the fall
seriously." By this he means that it is naive about the depth of evil in
the world and the ability of Christian love to overcome it. This criticism certainly holds true for those who think that the hearts of
bloody tyrants can always be melted by the witness of Christian
kindness. Again, however, it is not a valid objection to evangelical
theories of pacifism, which root loving one's enemy in the doctrine
of justification by faith and the total depravity of humankind.

A far more compelling criticism of Christian pacifism is that it
has a weak conception of justice. Theologian Oliver O'Donovan
advances this by suggesting that the word *war* confuses the debate,
as this word is hard to define. He says that the division between
war and domestic police work is misleading—both are about using
force to right wrongs. Certain crimes need to be addressed with
more force than others, and armed conflicts are crimes that need to
be rectified by armed conflict. If wars are thus seen as an extension
of the ordinary acts of judgment that police forces perform (sometimes with weapons), then pacifists must either condemn the police
and courts, leading to anarchy, or explain why they allow the police, but not soldiers, to use force. It is not clear that pacifists have
a robust answer to this objection, and it is rarely given sufficient
consideration in their writings.

The fourth criticism of pacifism is similarly better founded than the first two, and has attracted the most comment. In refusing to countenance the use of war to right wrongs, Christian pacifists allow injustice to continue, effectively sacrificing others for their personal moral purity and ignoring biblical injunctions to go out of our way to care for the weak, as the good Samaritan did. A. J. Coates puts it more forcefully still, stating that Christian pacifists become complicit in the harm or deaths of innocents. This is a weighty objection, as pacifism can indeed be an excuse for relieving oneself of the moral responsibility to others. However, this criticism is sometimes based on a confusion of the words *pacific* and *passive,* which sound similar in English but have no link in meaning. Late-twentieth-century Christian pacifism has accepted this challenge by developing theologies and practices of "active nonviolence," such as mass protests and behind-the-scenes conflict prevention and resolution. Advocates of Christian nonviolence claim that it has played a role in bringing down many unjust governments, and ending, calming or preventing numerous armed conflicts.

Two further criticisms of pacifism arise from this very turn to nonviolence. Nonviolent protests, refusals to cooperate with the regime, strikes, etc., can ratchet up the level of violence by provoking a government response, and may thus be hypocritical as part of a peace movement. Pacifists respond to this objection, as to the previous one, by observing that war itself does not always work, and the consequences of a failed military attempt to oppose injustice can be far more devastating than those of a failed campaign of nonviolence.

Twinned with this argument is another—that boycotting jobs can harm production output, which may contradict statements about loving one's enemies. For example, the civil rights movement's boycott of racially segregated buses and cafés no doubt harmed the livelihoods of white bus drivers and café owners. Reverend Martin Luther King Jr. countered this charge by leading the civil rights activists in prayers for the white oppressors, loving them by blessing not cursing and challenging black people who wanted to respond by violence. However, one might ask how different that is from St. Augustine's much-maligned sidestepping of the Sermon on the Mount by saying that Christians can love their enemies while slaying them in mortal combat, provided that they kill them in a just war with love, not hatred, in their hearts.

A seventh and final criticism of pacifism is that it confuses the political contexts of the gospels and the early church for later realities. Most just-war theorists would accept that Christ and the church fathers were, on the balance of evidence, pacifist. However, they would say that this was because of the context, and was not a blanket position to be adopted by every Christian community until Christ's return. Paul did not envisage a time when Christians were rulers in Rome rather than the persecuted. They would further contend that Christians should accept the opportunities for service and witness in states and their armed forces that early believers, who had no opportunity to join the military, did not have. As Martin Luther quipped, Christ's pacifism is no more binding on believers than his celibacy or his carpentry! Evangelical pacifists would reply that we should imitate Christ as the model for living our lives, and, as Scripture is the inspired Word of God and of relevance to all humankind, it cannot be claimed that the exhortations to follow Christ's example in this respect have been superseded by new political realities unforeseen by the New Testament writers.

Christian pacifism and just-war theory. The question of how Christians should respond to war is one that believers, perhaps especially those living in a democracy, cannot afford to ignore. The most enduring and coherent answers have been given by just-war theory and pacifism. It is not possible to say that either of these reigns supreme. There have been long periods where just-war theory has been in the ascendancy, such as the era of the crusades, and others where it has been almost forgotten in favor of pacifism, such as the periods either side of the crusades. Since World War II, there has been something of a revival in academic discussion of just-war theory, while pacifism has increasingly moved to the center stage of mainstream Protestant denominations and the Roman Catholic Church, and has eroded the influence of just-war theory. On balance, just-war theory has held more sway among theologians and church elites over time, but pacifism has always persisted, especially among ordinary Christians, and has often come to the foreground at times of religious revival or reform.

As stated earlier in the book, I consider that the weight of biblical evidence provides more support for Christian pacifism than for just-war theory. However, although the careful reader will no doubt be able to detect my position, it has not been the purpose of this book to make an argument for Christian pacifism over just-war theory. At best, both Christian pacifists and Christian just-war theorists are humble enough to accept that neither position is easy to adopt, as the consequences of both refraining from and engaging in war can be costly and terrible. In the final analysis, pacifism insists that the teachings of Christ take preeminence and are to be obeyed with the eye of faith, and that this imperative must override human reasoning such as pagan-based just-war theory. Just-war theorists, in turn, insist that this is a narrow reading of the ethics of Christ, and that, even though highly regrettable, violence is sometimes necessary to prevent or rectify injustice, and this consideration must override any apparent ethic of nonviolence in the New Testament. Undergirding both positions, however, is the belief that war is a departure from God's good purposes for humanity, that alternatives to war should be sought to resolve conflicts, and that the victory of Calvary will eventually be translated into ultimate and everlasting peace, when Jesus himself returns. It is important for brothers and sisters in Christ to remember this, and ensure that they enter into dialogue on this important topic in a spirit of love and humility. Pacifists can be surprisingly aggressive in their attacks on just-war theorists, who in turn can be very unjust in caricaturing and disparaging pacifists. That is ironic and unfortunate for interrelated positions that both espouse a commitment to peace and, more importantly, the Prince of Peace.

FOR FURTHER STUDY

A. J. Coates, *The Ethics of War* (Manchester, U.K.: Manchester University Press, 1997) is highly recommended as a general introduction to different approaches to war. Although not explicitly Christian, and largely dedicated to just-war theory (Coates's preference), the first section of the book contains an excellent critical discussion of just-war theory and pacifism. The second part of Coates's book is also very useful, with sections on the different criteria as set out in this study guide.

Joseph Fahey, *War and the Christian Conscience: Where Do You Stand?* (Maryknoll, N.Y.: Orbis, 2005) is the best work from a Christian viewpoint. Designed as a basic introduction, it clearly outlines the major traditions and relates them to each other, and it also has sections on how both just-war theory and pacifism relate to terrorism. Although Fahey leans toward Roman Catholic pacifism, his book is balanced and is even endorsed by a teacher at the United States Military Academy at West Point.

Charles Reed, *Just War?* (London: SPCK, 2004) uses just-war theory to analyze the Anglican church's position on Iraq from 1990 to 2003.

Written from a pacifist standpoint, Alan Kreider, *Journey To-wards Holiness: A Way of Living for God's Nation* (Scottdale, Penn.: Herald Press, 1987) is highly recommended. The book weaves Old and New Testament theology and church history together in a way that is highly accessible to the general reader, and it could serve as the basis for personal Bible studies.

John Yoder, *The Politics of Jesus* (1972; Carlisle, U.K.: Paternoster Press, 2000) remains the classic modern Christian pacifist text. Chapter two could be used as the basis for a series of Bible studies on selected episodes in Jesus' ministry from the Gospel of Luke. It would be interesting to contrast his reading of these passages with those of Bishop J. C. Ryle, *Luke*, 2 vols., Expository Thoughts on the Gospels (Edinburgh: Banner of Truth, 1998).

For group study. Using the seven debates and controversies about just-war theory and pacifism as a basis, arrange a group debate, with members adopting opposing positions and arguing their case for which is the most biblical approach. The aim of the debate is not necessarily to reach a consensus, but to air and develop the group members' opinions and thinking.

Christian Positions on the War on Terror

The first of these study guides discussed the meaning of terrorism and various political, largely secular, responses to the War on Terror. The second guide looked at general debates within the church about Christian responses to war, especially just-war theory and pacifism. This final study guide brings these together by looking at how Christians have responded to the War on Terror.

There have been numerous Christian responses to the War on Terror, far too many to summarize here. Although some people have described it as "a new kind of war," in fact, Christian responses have generally been framed in terms long established within the church, notably pacifism and just-war theory. (Holy-war responses from Christians, such as that of U.S. general William Boykin referred to in chapter two, have been marginal and roundly condemned by mainstream churches.) Pacifists have opposed military action but proposed different solutions to the problem of al-Qaeda. Just-war theorists have both opposed and supported the wars, and some who supported the Afghanistan invasion opposed the Iraq intervention. Both pacifists and just-war theorists have reconsidered aspects of their beliefs in the light of the War on Terror. The situation was even more complicated in church denominations, which often contained both pacifists and just-war theorists. Some churches called their members to join in the street demonstrations, some released reports and press statements, others sent delegations to lobby politicians while still others called on their members to support the wars. In general, it is probably fair to say that British churches (evangelical or otherwise) tended to be more critical of the war than American churches, and Christians in the rest of the world tended to be more critical than both their American and British counterparts. As time went by, British and American churches, too, became increasingly critical of aspects of the War on Terror.

In order to illustrate some of these debates, we will look at two well-known American spokespeople for the just-war and pacifist positions, Jean Bethke Elshtain and Jim Wallis. Their different positions reflect both their theologies and politics.

Jean Bethke Elshtain—A Just-War Response

A prominent Christian scholar who has used just-war theory to support the U.S. War on Terror is Jean Bethke Elshtain, a professor at the Chicago Divinity School. A noted public intellectual, her 2003 book, *Just War Against Terror: The Burden of American Power in a Violent World*, is a forthright defense of the War on Terror.

Professor Elshtain rails against what she considers left-wing opponents of the war. She laments the fact that in World War II, academics, including radicals, supported the U.S. war effort, but nowadays to oppose the War on Terror is almost a badge of honor. She thinks that those who argue that Osama bin Laden's goals are political are overlooking what he himself claims, shown by his call "on every Muslim who believes in Allah and wishes to be rewarded to comply with Allah's order to kill the Americans and plunder their money wherever and whenever they find it." She doubts that withdrawing U.S. forces from Saudi Arabia and other Muslim countries would satisfy radical Islamists, who "loathe us because of who we are and what our society represents." For this reason, too, she scorns the idea that poverty or the memory of the crusades is responsible for the September 11 attacks. Such arguments, she claims, are an insult to the poor and to Muslims, implying that they have no moral power to decide what is right and wrong and act accordingly. She thinks that this error of judgment is largely due to academics failing to appreciate the importance of religious motivation, and trying instead to find political reasons for everything. She also downplays claims about the harmful role of U.S. foreign policy, suggesting that it is not the force for bad in the world that many left-wing critics claim. Indeed, she praises the achievements of U.S. society and culture, contrasting it favorably with al-Qaeda's sheer "lust to dominate" and destroy, and the repression of Taliban-ruled Afghanistan that it so admired.

She is also very critical of how American churches have responded to terror. She says that concerns voiced about the impact of increased tensions on Christian minorities in Muslim countries, unreasonable demands for the U.S. to end poverty in the world instead of fight wars, and church statements protesting the attacks on Afghanistan and Iraq are seriously misguided.

Rather, she says, the churches should care primarily about justice and protecting the innocent from harm, which can be done in this context only by the use of military force. She laments that there has recently been "a falling away from the just-war tradition" in Christian thinking, in both Protestant and Catholic traditions. Rather, Professor Elshtain believes that the just-war tradition allows Christians to comment on, inform and support President Bush's wars. She considers that the War on Terror largely fulfills the criteria for a just war outlined in Study Guide 2. The attack on Afghanistan had a *just cause*—to prevent further harm and restore the necessary conditions for everyday peace in America and also in Afghanistan, where Taliban rule had led to oppression and poverty that made daily survival very difficult for the vulnerable. Restoring the right of women to gain education was an indication of how just the cause was. It had a *right intention*—to punish wrongdoers and prevent them from murdering more civilians. The war was conducted under *legitimate authority*—the U.S. Congress and Article 51 of the United Nations charter, recognizing the right of states to self-defense when attacked. U.S. military superiority gave more than a *reasonable chance of success*. Elshtain is less able to assert confidently that the war was a *last resort*, but observes that it was not begun immediately after September 11. She also argues that as Osama bin Laden was not a state or a recognized body, it is difficult to imagine what negotiations with him could have looked like anyway. Finally, she believes that the use of American military technology and tactics meant that the war was fought with both careful *discrimination* between legitimate and illegitimate targets, and that the *proportionate* level of force was used to achieve the U.S. goals.

Although her book was published before the invasion of Iraq, in an interview in March 2006 for America's Public Broadcasting Service, she indicated that she believes this too fulfilled the just-war criteria. Disarming weapons of mass destruction (which she assumes must have been smuggled out of the country because U.S. intelligence indicated that they had existed) constituted a *just cause*. More obviously, protecting innocent Iraqis from the brutality of Saddam Hussein was also a just cause, and the U.S. government, authorized by the Senate, had the *right authority* to do this. Although she thinks it is more doubtful whether the venture had a *reasonable chance of success*, she reckons on balance that it did. She also considers that, with few exceptions, the conduct of the wars has met the demands for *discrimination* and *proportionate response*, and abuses such as those at the Abu Ghraib prison are not

systematic, but the result of "one or two bad apples" in the barrel.
Elshtain is critical of scholars who suggest that the U.S. wars
lacked legality because they were not approved by the United Nations as the ultimate *right authority*. She argues that international
courts do not have legitimacy because they are not answerable to
or overseen by the parliaments of democratic states, and are weak
because they lack the means to enforce their decisions. Therefore,
America "must become the leading guarantor of a structure of sta-
bility and order in a violent world." She says that she is sympathetic to those who argue that America must embrace a new version
of imperialism for the good of the world, because America is the
only power strong enough to play that role, and because it is
founded on the principle of equality. She believes that Christians
should not oppose or hinder the U.S. role in this regard, but rather
are obliged to support it. She quotes Albert Camus, a famous
French atheist philosopher, who was angry at muted Christian condemnation of Nazism in parts of Europe. In 1948 he said that even
though he did not share the Christian hope, he had "the same revulsion from evil," and that the world "today needs Christians who
remain Christians" and oppose evil. In the same way, argues Elshtain, the world needs Christians to condemn terrorism unequivocally, and support the U.S. government in crushing it.

JIM WALLIS—A PACIFIST RESPONSE

An evangelical pacifist response to the War on Terror is articulated
by the former civil rights activist and prominent American evangelical leader Jim Wallis in his bestselling book, *God's Politics*. He argues that there are two great forces in the world today, the hunger
for spirituality and the desire for social change—forces that can be
brought together in a renewed evangelical Christianity reclaimed
from both right-wing extremists and liberals. Such a Christianity,

which is personal but not private, must speak prophetically to U.S. foreign policy—that is, it must articulate moral truth, diagnose the problem and offer a solution.

Wallis insists that Christians must not judge the president's foreign policy on whether they personally like or loathe him, but on the basis of Christian theology. On this ground, Wallis finds Bush's international policies wanting. He considers that the War on Terror correctly summons up the necessary resolve to respond to the horrific acts of September 11 but fails to provide moral and practical boundaries for a response. Indeed, he suggests that bombing campaigns against the populations of Kabul and Baghdad were acts of retribution that deprived the U.S. of the high moral ground, and acted as a recruiting sergeant for Osama bin Laden.

For Wallis, Bush's essential problem is theological. Wallis accepts the genuineness of President Bush's faith, but contends that in practice it works itself out as American nationalism rather than genuine Christianity. Bush's belief that God appointed him to be in charge of a good America to lead a righteous war to "rid the world of evil" on behalf of the hopes of all mankind is "a dangerous mix of bad foreign policy and bad theology." Wallis suggests that the abuse of detainees at Abu Ghraib prison can be traced directly to the White House's understanding of the War on Terror in simple theological terms of "good versus evil."

However, Jim Wallis is also critical of many on the political left. He says that some left-wing commentators have sounded like right-wing extremist Christians such as Jerry Falwell and Pat Robertson, blaming America for the attacks as if it deserved them. Whereas the extreme right said America was being punished for allowing sexual sin to go rampant, the extreme left implied that America got what it deserved on account of unjust foreign policies. Wallis says that there *is* a relationship between bin Laden's terror and U.S. foreign policy, but this evil is not the creation of American power, even if American power foolishly supported it. Likewise, global injustice is not the cause of terrorism (most of the oppressed do not become terrorists, whereas many members of the elite do), but it does provide a breeding ground for it, which must be addressed.

It is here he believes that Christian faith comes in: Jesus said that the peace*makers*, not peace*lovers,* are blessed, and actively making peace is at the heart of following Christ. Here, he contends, debates about pacifism and just-war theory are outdated, as they are of no practical use. A pacifism that does not go beyond protest and does not address the real threat of terrorists trying to kill thousands of innocents and take control of the Muslim world is not helpful; likewise, endless academic debates within just-war theory are not helping to prevent any wars, and the theory itself has been increasingly rendered obsolete due to changing military technology. Rather, he advocates "just peacemaking," transforming nonviolent initiatives that work to create practical, peaceful alternatives to injustice, by taking power and changing policy without recourse to violence. As an international community, the church is well placed to attempt this, and should also advocate multilateral resolution and prevention of conflict. He says that American Christians should not just oppose the invasion of Iraq, but should offer credible alternatives based on international law. Here, they should draw on what he sees as Micah's vision for national and global security, based on poverty reduction around the world, to address the injustices that propel many to terrorism.

RICHARD HORSLEY—AN ALTERNATIVE RESPONSE

The examples above fit into the just-war-theory/pacifism divide. However, there are alternative Christian responses that use different vocabularies and frame different ways of thinking about what is happening. To close this study guide, we will consider one example of these, the work of New Testament scholar Richard Horsley.

Jesus and empire. An innovative take on the Christian response to the War on Terror that uses the language of neither pacifism nor of just-war theory is Richard Horsley's comparison between first-century-Roman and twenty-first-century-American involvement in the Middle East. Because he does not advocate a position on the war but insists that the historical context of the Gospels must cause American Christians to engage in some profound reflection on the War on Terror, his ideas are worth considering in a category of their own. They are set forth most clearly in *Jesus and Empire: The Kingdom of God and the New World Disorder*, which builds on his earlier work, *Jesus and the Spiral of Violence: Popular Jewish Resistance in Roman Palestine* (Minneapolis: Fortress Press, 1992).

He traces the importance of the idea of Americans as a biblical people. From the early settlers who fled persecution in England, to later campaigns for slave emancipation, women's suffrage and black civil rights, Americans have frequently referred to the Bible, believing that God had delivered them from oppression to build a righteous and godly society. Indeed, U.S. policymakers from the founding fathers onward have tended to see themselves as playing a unique, God-given role in spreading divine civilization and liberation across the world. "Here then," wrote Reverend Thomas Brockaway in 1784 on the establishment of the United States, "is God erecting a stage on which to exhibit the great things of his kingdom." However, now the U.S. stands in the position of empire enforcing through military might a hegemony that is often resented. This is awkward for Americans contemplating their Christian origins, because Jesus of Nazareth carried out his mission in the midst of a Middle Eastern people who had been subject to Roman imperial rule.

Horsley argues that Roman rule of Palestine was exploitative and brutal. Rome maintained its control through local strongmen and governors such as Herod the Great, the priestly aristocracy and Pontius Pilate, with no legitimate channels left for popular political participation. As the Empire existed for economic appropriation performed by rulers with external support who did not therefore depend on popular legitimacy, exploitation grew and the traditional socioeconomic infrastructure broke down. Rising indebtedness of the peasantry to pay Roman and local taxes as well as temple tribute used by the ruling families led to growing social inequalities, dispossession of land and heavy indebtedness. Unsurprisingly, discontent and opposition mushroomed. Violent resistance to this oppression and injustice multiplied, leading to harsh repression and then revolt. This cycle of violence culminated in the massive revolt of A.D. 66-70.

Horsley sees in the teaching and example of Christ and the apostles both the indelible marks of this political context and resistance to this oppression. From Jesus' birth in Bethlehem (the result of a Roman census taken to enable taxation) through numerous parables and examples in his teaching, his clashes with the authorities and his ultimate execution as "the king of the Jews" by crucifixion (a horrific form of death reserved for *political* rebels), Horsley argues that Jesus, his followers and his opponents understood his mission as political. Likewise, Horsley contends, true to this mission, "Paul was, in effect, building an international anti-imperial movement of an alternative society based in local communities (*ekklesiai*)." Rome claimed to have in Caesar a "savior" who brought "peace and security," in whom people were meant to have "faith," a "Lord" who was to be honored in the assemblies (*ekklesiai*) of Roman cities. Much of Paul's terminology is borrowed from the Empire and turned back against imperial discourse, as Paul effectively declared Jesus to be the alternative, or real, emperor of the world who has passed judgment on corrupt and oppressive Roman rule (the "powers and authorities" referred to in 1 Corinthians 15:24, Colossians 2:15 and numerous other places). Little wonder, says Horsley, that Christians were persecuted by the Roman authorities for "defying Caesar's decrees, saying that there is another king" (Acts 17:7).

Jesus and Rome: Jesus and America. Horsley argues that U.S. Protestantism has failed to grasp the imperial context of the mission of Jesus and the forms of resistance to, and subversion of, Roman rule in the New Testament. On the contrary, he continues, it has rather distorted our understanding of the mission of Jesus by depoliticizing him and presenting him as a "personal savior" who came only to save souls and teach a private morality that does not apply to social contexts. This error, suggests Horsley, is due to a number of factors: first, the unwarranted reading back of modern assumptions about the separation of religion and politics, a modern idea that was absent from first-century Rome and Palestine; second, the Western ideology of individualism that sees Jesus as an individual independent of his social context; third, a tradition of liberal biblical criticism that sifted out judgmental claims and statements and reduced Jesus to a wandering hippy-type guru, purveying sayings and "spiritual" truths; fourth, modern New Testament scholarship that emerged in the heyday of European imperialism and portrayed the Roman Empire as a benign, civilizing framework for Christianity to emerge and spread. This ignored the horror and injustice of Roman rule as recorded in the Bible and in other histories, and gave a false impression of the political context of the Gospels.

This, suggests Horsley, leads to a coincidence between Roman and American rule in the Middle East, a comparison also drawn by geographer Simon Dalby. Just as the Roman Empire extracted grain and tribute from the Middle East, so the United States has extracted oil and sold weapons and other goods to Persian Gulf states. Both Rome and America have used a mixture of direct military intervention and alliances with local strongmen (Herod and Pilate for Rome; Saddam Hussein before 1991, and the royal families of Iran and Saudi Arabia for the United States) to cement their power. Whereas Rome "pacified" its frontiers through phalanxes of soldiers, ballistas, roads and galleys, the U.S. uses special forces, strategic bombers, airlift capabilities and aircraft carriers. Like Rome, the U.S. has collaborated with local (irregular) forces and stationed garrisons to support local rulers. Roman rule frequently led to dissatisfaction and acts of violence, just as the U.S. presence has engendered numerous terrorist attacks, from the killing of 243 marines in Beirut in 1983 to the 9/11 attacks themselves. Conceived thus, the War on Terror is not a new war, but yet another example of a counter-insurgency operation on the fringes of empire.

Horsley concludes by insisting that this comparison, based on the coincidence of resistance to Roman and American power in the Middle East, should make American Christians ponder again their role in the world. He says that 9/11 must make them revise any idea about a depoliticized Jesus. Although historically understanding themselves as playing a special role in God's purposes of spreading light and liberty around the world, American Christians find themselves as part of a country perpetrating the type of oppression that their Lord Jesus Christ suffered under and resisted. Horsley thus concludes with a call for Americans to reconsider the contradiction between their cultural scriptural heritage and their "own situation and roles in the current new world disorder established by the combination of American political power and the power of global capitalism."

Questions must be asked about how historically valid Richard Horsley's comparison between Rome and the United States is, but it is a comparison that both advocates and opponents of U.S. intervention in Afghanistan and Iraq have drawn for very different ends. Nonetheless, it represents an increasingly influential school of biblical scholarship that surely provides Christians with much food for thought as they contemplate the question of what Jesus would do in the War on Terror. It is impossible for us to answer that conclusively, and unwise for any Christian to claim that they know the mind of God on this topic. Horsley, however, would perhaps argue that it is better to ask "what *did* Jesus do?" when faced with a similar situation—a question that can be answered, and that can inform reflection on our own times.

CONCLUSION

Two factors have shaped Christian responses to the War on Terror. The first is debate about the relationship between Islamist terrorism and U.S./Western foreign policy, in which broadly left-right political divisions can be detected. The second is the basic positions that Christians have taken in response to war over the centuries, especially just-war theory and pacifism. Together, these have informed Christian reactions to the War on Terror. War does not present a new theological problem to Christians, but each new war presents challenges in the way that Christians have to think through their established positions. Evangelical Christians claim that the gospel is God's answer to sin, and the Bible our surest guide for life. If that is the case, and if war is a result of the fall of mankind into sin, then we need to apply ourselves diligently to the study of Scripture, and consistently apply its lessons to what is going on in our world. Only then will we be able to live as Christians through the War on Terror.

FOR FURTHER STUDY

Stephen Mansfield, *The Faith of George W. Bush* (New York: Jeremy P. Tarcher/Penguin, 2003) considers the place of Christian faith in President Bush's life, although it is more of a eulogy than a biography.

Jean Bethke Elshtain, *Just War Against Terror: The Burden of American Power in a Violent World* (New York: Basic Books, 2003).

Jim Wallis, *God's Politics: Why the Right Gets It Wrong and the Left Doesn't Get It* (San Francisco: Harper One, 2005).

For a good collection of short essays by a variety of Christian writers, see Jon Berquist, ed., *Strike Terror No More: Theology, Ethics, and the New War* (St. Louis, Mo.: Chalice Press, 2002).

Richard Horsley, *Jesus and Empire: The Kingdom of God and the New World Disorder* (Minneapolis: Fortress Press, 2003) contains a historical outline of the New Testament's political context and will help Christians understand the backdrop of the Gospel narratives better. (See also Simon Dalby's academic article "Calling 911: Geopolitics, Security and America's New War," *Geopolitics* 8, no. 3 [2003], pp. 61-86.)

William Willimon published a moving collection of short sermons preached in American college chapels on the week of the September 11 attacks—*The Sunday After Tuesday: College Pulpits Respond to 9/11* (Nashville: Abingdon Press, 2002). The preachers advocate a variety of positions, from just-war to pacifism, but all seek to address the terrible events of that week in the light of Scripture.

Taking This Further

In addition to the suggestions for private and group study, there are many ways in which churches can take this topic further, such as:

- Encourage pastors and preachers to address the topic.
- Arrange church discussion groups, inviting speakers with knowledge or experience in the subject.
- Set aside Sunday services, with prayers, Bible reading, songs and sermons reflecting coherently on the theme of war and peace.
- Organize church retreats or weekends away around this theme.
- Find out about the work of an initiative organized by your denomination or other Christians, and support it in prayer and financial giving.
- Strengthen your church's sense of being part of the transnational church by making contact with Christians in a country that your country is in conflict with, learning about their needs and experiences and how you can support each other. Do this by reaching out to people from other countries who live in your home area—not only other Christians, but groups such as refugees.
- Hold public discussions and talks about Christianity and war and peace, organized in such a way as to draw outsiders in to engage with the church on a topic that they are interested in. You may

decide it is best to hold them in venues other than church buildings, and to promote them in the local press and community.

- In place of standard summer holidays, encourage church members, where appropriate, to visit and thereby support the work
  of Christians involved in peacemaking in troubled parts of the
  world.

The possibilities are exciting and endless. You are welcome to
contact the author, by e-mail at <N.W.Megoran.97@cantab.net> or
via InterVarsity Press, to discuss any ideas further.

Notes

Chapter 1: Introduction: Living as Christians Through the War on Terror

[1]D. Martyn Lloyd-Jones, *Why Does God Allow War?* (Wheaton, Ill.: Crossway, 2003).

[2]George Bell, "The Church's Function in Wartime," in *The Church and Humanity* (London: Longman, Green & Co., 1946).

Chapter 3: "Love Your Enemies"—Even After September 11?

[1]D. A. Carson, *Love in Hard Places* (Wheaton, Ill.: Crossway, 2002).

[2]Miroslav Volf, *Exclusion and Embrace: A Theological Exploration of Identity, Otherness, and Reconciliation* (Nashville: Abingdon Press, 1996).

[3]Jürgen Moltmann, *The Power of the Powerless* (London: SCM, 1983).

[4]Robin Lane Fox, *Pagans and Christians* (New York: Knopf, 1987).

Chapter 4: Why Does God Allow War and Terrorism?

[1]Elie Wiesel, "Jeremiah," in *Five Biblical Portraits* (Notre Dame, Ind.: University of Notre Dame Press, 1981).

[2]D. Martyn Lloyd-Jones, *Why Does God Allow War?* (Wheaton, Ill.: Crossway, 2003). See also D. Martyn Lloyd-Jones, *A Nation Under Wrath: Studies in Isaiah 5* (Eastbourne, U.K.: Kingsway, 1997).

[3]Richard France tells Henry Martyn's life story in *Five Pioneer Missionaries*, ed. S. Houghton (London: Banner of Truth, 1965).

[4]John Sargent, ed., *The Life and Letters of Henry Martyn* (Edinburgh: Banner of Truth, 1985).

Chapter 5: Living with Two Passports

[1] Quintin Hogg, Baron Hailsham of St. Marylebone, *The Door Wherein I Went* (London: Collins, 1975).

[2] Renny Golden and Michael McConnell, *Sanctuary: The New Underground Railroad* (Maryknoll, N.Y.: Orbis, 1986).

[3] André Trocmé's work during World War II is reported by Philip Hallie, *Lest Innocent Blood Be Shed* (London: Michael Joseph, 1979).

Chapter 6: A Tale of Two Cities: Nationalism, Terrorism and Reconciliation

[1] G. K. Chesterton, *The Napoleon of Notting Hill* (London: Bodley Head, 1904).

[2] Robert Pape, *Dying to Win: The Strategic Logic of Suicide Terrorism* (New York: Random House, 2005).

[3] Alan and Eleanor Kreider, *Becoming a Peace Church* (London: New Ground, 2000).

[4] Clifford Longley, *Chosen People: The Big Idea that Shaped England and America* (London: Hodder & Stoughton, 2002).

[5] Gregory Baum, "The Role of the Church in Polish-German Reconciliation," in *The Reconciliation of Peoples: Challenge to the Churches,* ed. Gregory Baum and Harold Wells (Maryknoll, N.Y.: Orbis, 1997).

Chapter 7: Learning to Be Peacemakers—in the Church and in the World

[1] Aldous Huxley, *The Human Situation: Lectures at Santa Barbara, 1959* (London: Chatto & Windus, 1980).

[2] R. B. Kuiper, *The Glorious Body of Christ* (London: Banner of Truth, 1967).

[3] Alan and Eleanor Kreider, *Becoming a Peace Church* (London: New Ground, 2000).

[4] Peter Oakes, *Philippians: From People to Letter* (Cambridge: Cambridge University Press, 2001).

[5] Dylan Mathews, *War Prevention Works: 50 Stories of People Resolving Conflict* (Oxford: Oxford University Press, 2001).

Chapter 8: The Battle of Jericho and the London Bombs

[1] Christopher Hitchens, *Letters to a Young Contrarian* (New York: Basic Books, 2001).

[2] John G. Paton's biography is related by John Legg in *Five Pioneer Missionar-*

ies, ed. S. Houghton (London: Banner of Truth, 1965).

[3]Tom Skinner recounts his story in *Words of Revolution* (Devon, U.K.: Paternoster, 1970).

[4]Alice Hoare, *The Fire that Burned in the Life of Dorothy Hoare: For Thirty Years Ambassador for Christ in Japan* (published privately, n.d.).

[5]Bishop J. C. Ryle, *Matthew,* Expository Thoughts on the Gospels (1856; Edinburgh: Banner of Truth, 1986).

Chapter 9: After Beslan: "The Cords of Death Entangled Me"

[1]The story of Sarah Carson in Haiti is recounted in John Howard Yoder, *What Would You Do? If a Violent Person Threatened to Harm a Loved One . . .* (Scottdale, Penn.: Herald Press, 1992).

[2]Kefa Sempangi's autobiography is *Reign of Terror, Reign of Love: A Firsthand Account of Life and Death in Idi Amin's Uganda* (Tring, U.K.: Lion, 1979).

[3]For more information on the involvement of Christians in the end of the Cold War, see Michael MccGwire, *Perestroika and Soviet National Security* (Washington, D.C.: The Brookings Institution, 1991).

[4]For more on Dorothy Day, see Eileen Egan, *Peace Be with You: Justified Warfare or the Way of Nonviolence* (Maryknoll, N.Y.: Orbis, 2000).

[5]The suffering and response of Christians in Beslan is retold by Dawn Herzog Jewell in the article "Praying for Terrorists. Christians Seek Healing in Beslan" in *Christianity Today* (November 2004)—also available at <http://www.christianitytoday.com/ct/2004/november/1.19.html>.

Chapter 10: Who Is Winning the War on Terror?

[1]On President George W. Bush's 2002 National Security Strategy, see Wes Avram, ed., *Anxious About Empire: Theological Essays on the New Global Realities* (Grand Rapids: Brazos Press, 2004). The book reprints the full text of the strategy, and contains a number of theological responses to it.

[2]Ravi Zacharias, quoting from Malcolm Muggeridge, *The Veritas Forum at Harvard University* (3 tapes).

[3]See Tricia Gates Brown, ed., *Getting in the Way: Stories from Christian Peacemaker Teams* (Scottdale, Penn.: Herald Press, 2005).

Chapter 11: Christian Hope and Suicide Bombers

[1]This analysis of optimism and stoicism is based on D. Martyn Lloyd-Jones in

his book on 2 Timothy 1:12, *I Am Not Ashamed* (1986; London: Hodder & Stoughton, 1994).

[2]For a biography of Horatio Spafford, see the Library of Congress website for "the American Colony in Jerusalem" exhibition <http://www.loc.gov/exhibits /americancolony/amcolony-family.html>.

[3]In response to this tragedy, in 1881 Horatio and Anna Spafford moved to Jerusalem and founded the American Colony, which undertook philanthropic work and gained the trust of all faith communities. Although the Colony no longer exists, their headquarters still serve as a meeting place. In 1992 representatives from the Palestinian Liberation Organization and Israel met there to begin talks that led to the historic 1993 Oslo Peace Accord.

[4]For Reverend Mehdi Dibaj's testimony and a brief biography, see "The Written Defense of the Rev. Mehdi Dibaj Delivered to the Sari Court of Justice— Sari, Iran, December 3, 1993" <http://www.farsinet.com/dibaj/>, accessed September 2006.